CHRISTIANITY

in

MODERN THEOLOGY

Cornelius Van Til
Westminster Theological Seminary
Philadelphia, Penna.

MACK PUBLISHING COMPANY
Cherry Hill, N. J.

For of him, and through him, and to him, are all things: to whom be glory for ever.
Romans 11:36

First printing, 1955

Reprinted, 1973

PREFACE

From time to time I have written reviews of current books on apologetical subjects. Only books of more than passing importance were discussed. For that reason it was thought to be useful to have these reviews republished and made available in one volume. Each of the included reviews originally appeared in the *Westminster Theological Journal*.

Cornelius Van Til

Philadelphia
September, 1955

TABLE OF CONTENTS

REVIEWS OF BOOKS

Emil Brunner: *Der Mensch im Widerspruch*. Berlin: Furche-Verlag. 1937. xv, 572. Rm. 12.80.

Emil Brunner is one of the leading theologians of our day. He represents what is frequently spoken of as *Crisis Theology*. This crisis theology has made a vigorous attack on Modernism. Brunner and Barth have called men back to what they call the "theology of the Reformation". We cannot help but be interested in it.

Brunner's recent book, *Der Mensch im Widerspruch*, deals with the doctrine of man. It speaks a good deal of man's creation in the image of God and of his fall into sin. This naturally brings forward the problem of history. Does Brunner accept the Genesis account of man's creation and fall at face value? Up to this time Reformed theologians have done this. Brunner's predecessors in the chair of systematic theology at Princeton have done this. They have held that the Scriptures as the Word of God and historic Christianity itself would fall to the ground unless the Genesis account be taken as literally true.

We need not read far into Brunner's book to find that it is at odds with the Reformed and generally orthodox conception of history. Brunner's philosophy of history resembles that of Kant. Kant made a broad distinction between the realm of *phenomena* and the realm of *noumena*; Brunner makes a broad distinction between the *dimension of Becoming* and the *dimension of History*. Generally speaking Brunner's dimension of Becoming answers to Kant's phenomena while Brunner's dimension of History answers to Kants' noumena. The dimension of Becoming deals with causal sequences and necessary relations. It is therefore open to scientific research. The dimension of History, or rather real-history, (die Echtgeschichtliche) deals with events not repeatable (das Einmalige). True historical narrative is therefore descriptive, not explanatory.[1]

Traditional or orthodox theology, says Brunner, has failed to make the all-important distinction between the dimension of Becoming and that of

[1] P. 412. "Dass das Echtgeschichtliche gerade nicht das Werdende als solches ist, geht daraus hervor, dass es das Einmalige ist."

History. What Scripture tells us about man's creation and fall into sin is History. It therefore does not belong to the dimension of Becoming. "The contrast 'created good . . . fallen' has nothing to do with the distinction 'earlier . . . later' in the field of empirical sequence" (p. 413). The creation and the fall of man are not occurrences in the empirical realm, the realm of Becoming. The creation and the fall lie behind or above the level of the empirical. Yet traditional theology has taken the Genesis narrative as referring to the realm of Becoming. The consequences, he thinks, have been sad indeed.

Traditional theology has, according to Brunner, made itself ridiculous by clinging to the literal interpretation of the Genesis account (p. 76). It has wasted its energies in a useless struggle with science. It has engaged in a fruitless apologetic for the Christian Faith (p. 440).

A "purified theology", says Brunner, must follow a different procedure (p. 416). It must recognize the fact of organic evolution as practically beyond dispute (pp. 407, 434). It must not enter upon the dimension of Becoming in order there to engage in a debate with science. For information on questions of anatomy and chemistry a true theology turns to science, not to Scripture. The biological, the psychological and even the intellectual aspects of man answer to definite laws. Science, not Scripture informs us of the operation of these laws (p. 58).

A true theology, says Brunner, will limit itself to what Scripture tells us of the dimension of History. That dimension is the dimension of personality. It is here that man is responsible and responsibility is of the essence of man (p. 38). It is here too that man is brought face to face with other persons. Here the *I* meets the *Thou* (p. 10). The relationship of one person to another person is not by way of their common membership in the same species. The notion of a species is that of a universal and universals belong to the dimension of Becoming. Science may approach the idea of personality with the help of universals but personality is in the last analysis absolutely unique.

We pause to observe the close affinity of Brunner's thought to that of Kant on this point. Both hold to a deep gulf between the domain of science and the domain of free personality. Then, to soften the resulting dualism, both introduce the notion of the limiting concept (Grenzbegriff). Those who do not accept the Christian conception of history are driven to invent devices of this sort. If the "facts" of the phenomenal world — Brunner's dimension of Becoming — are not thought of as created by God they must be thought of as existing in their own power. Brunner, as will be shown later, does not really believe in the creation of the "facts" of the phenomenal world by God. Thus they are "brute facts". And brute facts are mute facts. They are unintelligible. Granted the mind of man can know aspects of these facts, there is always a remaining surd. Granted man by science can discover certain laws of behavior in the realm of phenomena, the individual fact in its uniqueness must always recede as does the horizon. Kant's philosophy and Brunner's philosophy end in modern irrationalism.

Brunner insists again and again that human responsibility cannot be maintained if one fails to make the distinction between the dimension of Becoming and the dimension of History as he has made it. He charges traditional theology with obscuring the true Biblical doctrine of origins. The Scriptural doctrine of creation, he says, was meant to teach man's utter dependence upon God. But our descent from Adam in paradise would drag responsibility down into the dimension of Becoming. The church has toned down our individual responsibility to God by mediating it, in part at least, through mere physical descent.[4]

Similarly, says Brunner, traditional theology has obscured the Biblical notion of man's creation in the image of God. To be created in the image of God means to be personally and immediately related to Christ the Word and thus to be immediately responsible to God (p. 87. Also, p. 95). But the church has toned down this individual dialectical relationship to the level of generic possession of certain attributes (p. 94). True History has again been confused with mere Becoming.

Still further, the church, according to Brunner, has obscured the Biblical doctrine of the fall of man. Sin should be thought of as something purely personal and therefore individual. Sin is, in the last analysis, an act of the free personality. But the church has reduced personality to the level of membership in a species. Thus individual responsibility has been virtu ally denied. "Something, which in its very nature is purely personal: sin disobedience to the will of God, has been reduced to the purely natur fact of physical descent" (p. 113). Thus it would appear that the fall of

---

[4] P. 76. Also p. 78, "Durch diese Neuformulierung wird vor allem erst deutlich gemacht, dass, wo vom Ursprung die Rede ist, nicht von irgen deinem Adam, der vor so und so viel tausend Jahren lebte, die Rede ist sondern von mir selbst, ebenso von dir selbst und von jedem selbst."

man is something that lies behind us in the dim past, something for which a certain individual named Adam, was responsible. In reality we are all responsible; we are all Adam (p. 144). In the dimension of History there are no causal relations between individuals and therefore no transfer of responsibility from one person to another.

We see that Brunner's charges against traditional theology are very severe. He proposes to reconstruct traditional theology with the help of his distinction between Becoming and History. With the help of this distinction a really Christian theology is to be built up. It is with the help of this distinction that human responsibility is to be given a true foundation. Will Brunner accomplish his purpose? We believe not.

Modern philosophers and theologians who have followed Kant in making his distinction between phenomena and noumena have been unable to escape the notion of a finite God. The God they believed in was limited in a twofold fashion.

He was limited, in the first place, by the phenomena. These phenomena, or "facts", were assumed to exist in themselves. They were thought of as non-created. Their laws were independent of the providence of God. God had to adjust Himself to the facts as He found them. In His knowledge of these facts he was essentially on a par with the scientists. Both had to await developments. Neither could do more than approximate to a knowledge of facts as they are.

God was also limited, in the second place, by the noumena. The inhabitants of the noumenal world too were non-created. God had to await the actions of the *homo noumenon*. The *homo noumenon* of Kant was the hypostatisation of human thought conceived of as self-sufficient. Thus man was, in the last analysis, responsible not to God but to abstract laws which he found operating within himself. God as well as man was surrounded by an ultimately impersonalistic universe.

Brunner's God, like the God of Kant, is really no more than a limited God. At certain points in his book it might seem as though he were using the word creation in the traditional sense of the term but the full impact of his argument is against the creation idea. For Brunner the idea of creation conveys no information about the origin of the physical universe as such. Thus the facts and the laws of the phenomenal world are virtually beyond the control of God. Fate or Chance may rule over them.

We are aware of the fact that Brunner criticises both pantheism and deism with the help of the creation doctrine (p. 80). But to escape from these enemies of the Christian faith one must take the creation doctrine seriously. The Reformation theology did take creation seriously. Kant took the creation doctrine metaphorically. Brunner has followed Kant, not Luther or Calvin.

Brunner's distinction between the dimension of Becoming and the dimension of History removes the foundation of historic Christianity. For him nothing of real importance to Christianity happens in the dimension of Becoming.[5] He leaves no room for the all-determinative significance of the death and resurrection of Christ. He leaves no place for miracle without which redemption falls to the ground. Every part of Christian doctrine would have to be modified, or rather volatalized, if Brunner's philosophy of history were true.

The root error of Brunner's theology, we believe, lies in his assumption of the ultimacy of man. The key-word of his book is "Entscheidung". Man must make his choice for or against God. Now Brunner assumes that man must virtually be a self-sufficient being in order to make a significant choice. As Brunner's dimension of History is broadly similar to Kant's noumenal realm so his notion of human freedom is closely related to that of Kant. As a member of the dimension of History man is, according to Brunner, free from all entangling alliances with the dimension of Becoming. He is a citizen in the field of absolute personality.

Further we are aware of the fact that Brunner speaks of man as a creature of God (p. 80, and elsewhere). But this is really no more than metaphor. It is an undeniable fact that man's choices are to a large extent influenced by what Brunner calls the dimension of Becoming. If this dimension of Becoming is withdrawn from God's control man's choices are to that extent withdrawn from God's control. We are face to face here with an ultimate alternative. Either we take the doctrine of creation and of providence seriously and have man's real dependence upon God or we do not take them seriously and we have something similar to Kant's *homo noumenon*.

The alternative spoken of has controlled the history of philosophy and theology. On the one hand we have paganism or ultimate impersonalism. On the other hand we have Christianity or ultimate personalism. For paganism the Universe is logically prior to God; God is reduced to an aspect of the Universe. Together with man God is subject to the laws of the

[5] P. 458. "Auf dem Feld empirischen Geschehens fallen keine endgültigen Entscheidungen."

Universe. Man can at any time appeal from God's verdict to the constitution of the Universe. This constitution of the universe is as a "daysman betwixt them both". For Christianity God is logically prior to the universe; God's counsel controls all that which influences man. There are no "facts" or "laws" that operate independently of God. Even the "dimension of Becoming" exists and functions only by virtue of God's creating and sustaining power. Thus God is really sovereign. Man may deal with facts and laws but through them he always deals with God. In all that man touches he either obeys or disobeys the will of God.

Brunner has apparently sought to combine the pagan and the Christian motifs. There are many fine passages in his book that criticise the impersonalism of modern theology. Our hopes are again and again aroused when he scourges Modernism for its reduction of historic Christianity to a mere ideational system of thought. In eloquent phrases he chastises the pride of the modern *homo noumenon*. But in the last analysis Brunner falls into the errors he so passionately condemns. By his false notion of creation he withdraws the universe in which man dwells from the control of God. Thus man's responsibility is directed to abstract law and man is himself made the judge of that law. Pagan ideationism reigns supreme and *homo noumenon* is still upon the throne.

Brunner has no patience with traditional Apologetics. We may fairly request him then to make intelligible to us his own philosophy of human personality. He cannot escape doing so by saying that his interest is in theology and not in philosophy. His own criticisms of traditional theology are philosophical in nature. His entire scheme of Biblical interpretation — the distinction between Becoming and History — is taken from modern philosophy. The influence of Kant, Fichte, Kierkegaard, Heidegger and others, appears on every page.

In defending his philosophy Brunner will have to prove that human responsibility is intelligible upon the presupposition of an ultimately impersonalistic universe. But an impersonalistic universe is, when analyzed, a Chance universe, and Chance spells the death of intelligible predication. In a Chance universe no two facts can be brought into significant contact with one another.

Brunner's theology is destructive of historic Christianity; his Apologetic destroys human intelligence itself. In contrast with this the Reformed Faith, in accepting the creation doctrine in its ordinary sense has a basis for historic Christianity and has an apologetic which alone does not destroy human intelligence. The Reformed Faith does not claim to fathom the depth of the wisdom of God. It offers no apologetic in which the *homo noumenon* is the last court of appeal. It holds to the sovereign God, Creator and Ruler of all. To Him, and to Him alone, in the end is man responsible. Thus alone we do justice to plain Scripture teaching; thus alone we can save human responsibility and intelligible human predication. God is the presupposition of intelligible human predication.

If we could speak of Brunner's theology as orthodox we should have to call it Arminian but we cannot call it Arminian because it is in no real sense orthodox. The presuppositions of Brunner's theology are the same as those of Modernism. Much as we bewail this fact we ought to face it squarely.

REVIEWS OF BOOKS

ed. Paul Arthur Schilpp: *The Philosophy of Alfred North Whitehead* (The Library of Living Philosophers, Volume III). Evanston and Chicago: Northwestern University. 1941. xx, 745. $4.00.

The Philosophy of Alfred North Whitehead constitutes the third volume of "The Library of Living Philosophers". The first volume dealt with the philosophy of Dewey and the second with that of Santayana. "The Library of Living Philosophers", as this volume shows afresh, serves a very useful purpose. Unfortunately Professor Whitehead was unable to offer the customary "Reply" to the evaluations of his philosophy the present volume contains. In lieu of a "Reply" we find "his two most recent philosophical papers and utterances: papers concerning which he himself writes that they 'summarize' his 'final point of view' and constitute, to his own mind, a sufficient answer to his questioners and critics" (p. xv).

We cannot deal fully with the wealth of material this volume places before us. It is with the picture as a whole that we shall be concerned. Difficult as it remains, even after the admirable work bestowed upon this volume, to obtain a rounded view of the philosophy of Whitehead, we must attempt to say something about it.

Whitehead's philosophy, it appears anew from this volume, is primarily a "process philosophy". In this respect it is very similar to that of Alexander, for whose work he expresses an admiration (*Science and the Modern World*, New York, 1926, p. xi), and to that of Bergson to whom he considers himself indebted. Whitehead calls his particular variety of process philosophy the "Philosophy of Organism".

The "Philosophy of Organism" seeks to avoid the "fallacy of misplaced concreteness". This fallacy, Whitehead says, is imbedded in the Cartesian tradition of science and philosophy. The "fallacy of misplaced concreteness", he argues, was due to false intellectual abstraction from experience. By means of this false abstraction from experience men absolutized entities so as to deprive them of all relevance to daily life. They indulged in the idea of "vacuous actualities". The "world of becoming" was "managed from without" by a Stage Manager called God. Scientists worked with "the ancient trinity of time, space and matter" (p. 66) and spoke of each of them as ultimates (See, also, *Science and the Modern World*, pp. 74 ff.). Says Whitehead: "Newtonian physics is based upon the independent individuality of each bit of matter. Each stone is conceived as fully describable apart from any reference to any other portion of matter. It might be alone in the Universe, the sole occupant of uniform space. But it would still be that stone which it is. Also the stone could be adequately described without any reference to past or future. It is to be conceived fully and adequately as wholly constituted within the present moment" (*Adventures of Ideas*, New York, 1933, pp. 200 f.).

Whitehead's philosophy is negatively critical of this doctrine of "simple location", this "bifurcation of nature". The Century of Genius, he argues, forgot that the "notion of a mere fact is the triumph of the abstractive intellect" (*Modes of Thought*, Cambridge, 1938, p. 12). "A single fact in isolation" is, to be sure, "the primary myth required for finite thought, that is to say, for thought unable to embrace totality" (*Ibid.*), but in reality there is no such fact. "No fact is merely itself." He argues that "in every consideration of a single fact there is the suppressed presupposition of the environmental coördination requisite for its existence" (*Idem*, p. 13). "In the nature of things there are no ultimate exclusions, expressive in logical terms" (*Idem*, p. 76).

It is Whitehead's aim to overcome all dualism. Traditional modern physics, he says, has bequeathed to philosophy an epistemological impasse that cannot be adequately met unless we insist relentlessly on the primacy of process. Only thus can we correct the fallacy of misplaced concreteness (p. 470). " 'Nothing is finally understood until its reference to process has been made evident' " (p. 568). Process is "the on-going of the universe" (*Ibid.*). If we insist on the primacy of process we see things as they are. Experience knows nothing of mere facts in an order of observation or of abstract universals in an order of conceptualization. All ultimate facts are *events* (Dorothy M. Emmet, *Whitehead's Philosophy of Organism*, p. 78). A fact without its "historic route" is a nonentity. "The final problem is to conceive a complete fact" (*Adventures of Ideas*, p. 203).

The fundamental notions in terms of which we are to seek for the idea of a complete fact are set forth in Whitehead's great work on *Process and Reality*. He himself has summarized these notions for us as follows:

"The temporal world and its formative elements constitute for us the all-inclusive universe. These formative elements are:

1. The creativity whereby the actual world has its character of temporal passage to novelty.

2. The realm of ideal entities, or forms, which are in themselves not actual, but are such that they are exemplified in everything that is actual, according to some proportion of relevance.

3. The actual but non-temporal entity whereby the indetermination of mere creativity is transmuted into determinate freedom. This non-temporal actual entity is what men call God — the supreme God of rationalized religion."[1]

These basic concepts, as Victor Lowe puts it, "are intended to be so inclusive in scope, and so interlocked, as to overcome all the classical dualisms of metaphysics: mind and matter, God and the world, permanence and transience, causality and teleology, atomism and continuity, sensation and emotion, internal and external relations, etc., as well as subject and object" (pp. 106 f.). To begin with, we have the protean character of creativity as such. Due to its persistent and pervasive influence the universe is open and remains open. The temporal world, says Whitehead, "is an essential incompleteness". This notion of bare possibility is fundamental to all Whitehead's thought. Secondly, we have the notion of "eternal objects" or abstract universals. These forms have no independent ontological status; they are to be understood in a genetic-functional manner. By these forms the human mind creates finite order in the infinite chaos. The notions of infinite possibility and the finite categorising activity of the human mind involve one another and are meaningless without one another. "The notion of the essential relatedness of all things is the primary step in understanding how finite entities require the unbounded universe, and how the universe acquires meaning and value by reason of its embodiment of the activity of finitude" (pp. 674 f.).

It is difficult to determine the place of God in Whitehead's philosophy. When he has an ultimate creativity plus the forming activity of the human mind, he seems to have all the factors he needs for his "Philosophy of Organism". Individuality seems to be provided by creativity and connectedness seems to be provided by the forms. Indeed, Whitehead frequently writes as though this is all that is needed for an explanation of experience. This is the case, for instance, in his lecture on "Mathematics and the Good", which forms part of "The Philosopher's Summary" at the end of the book under discussion. "The crux of philosophy", he says, "is to retain the balance between the individuality of existence and the relativity of existence" (p. 680). But these requirements are met, he seems to think, if the human mind in its generalising activity, exhibited particularly in mathematics, imposes its pattern upon the original indeterminate

[1] *Religion in the Making*, New York, 1926, p. 90.

infinitude. By the correlativity of the two factors of pure creativity and the patternizing function of human experience Whitehead seems to provide, on the one hand, for "sheer individuality" and, on the other hand, for "essential relativity". Yet Charles Hartshorne holds that Whitehead's is the "first great systematic philosophy" that leads "naturally and consistently to the religious idea of God" (p. 516).

To be useful and necessary in philosophy, God must not be conceived, Hartshorne argues, either as "sheer absolute perfection" or as "sheer causality or actuality" (p. 517). "It has been too lightly assumed that God's perfection must be all of one kind, without contrast or categorical distinction" (p. 519). We must rather distinguish between the primordial and the consequent natures of God (p. 525). The primordial nature of God is, says Hartshorne, quoting Whitehead's words, " 'limited by no actuality which it presupposes' ". It is " 'complete, perfect, infinite' ". The consequent nature is said to be "relative, incomplete, and in flux" (p. 525). What purpose does such a God serve in the categorial scheme of Whitehead's philosophy? In answer to this question we quote from Hartshorne:

"To the question, Why after all is there a conception of God in Whitehead's philosophy? the answer is two-fold. First, Whitehead is not without religion. Second, his categories, adopted at least as much for other purposes, require God as their 'chief' and indispensable exemplification" (p. 535).

A little later he adds:

"How do Whitehead's categories require a supreme example? There are as many answers as there are categories; for they all require God. (1) Possibility implies a supreme and primordial ground, (2) actuality an all-inclusive actual entity, (3) the transition (creativity) from possibility to actuality a supreme creative agent, (4) memory a highest type of retention of elapsed events, (5) purpose and love a highest or perfect type of purpose and love, and (6) order a supreme ordering factor" (p. 536).

This argument of Hartshorne is far from conclusive. We have seen that Whitehead himself reduces all his categorial distinctions to three that are basic. The "primary actual units of which the temporal world is composed", often called the "epochal occasions", are said to be what they are because of these three basic categories. "The various elements which are thus brought into unity are the other creatures and the ideal forms and God" (*Religion in the Making*, p. 93). And of these three God has least to do. In fact he seems to have nothing to do. He is, it would seem, to use Hartshorne's expression, nothing but the great exemplification of the Process of the Universe. That is to say, he is the pictorial representation of that Process in the minds of men. The transition from the primordial to the consequent nature of God is virtually identical with the Process of the Universe. The primordial nature of God in itself involves no consciousness (See Newton P. Stallknecht, *Studies in the Philosophy of Creation*, Princeton, 1934, p. 144). "It is only the consequent nature that recognizes and cherishes concretions" (*Idem*, p. 145). We must remember, says Stallknecht, that for Whitehead the "final plunge into actuality, the 'decision of the subject-superject' is beyond any domination" (*Idem*, p. 146). Out of this plunge into actuality personality finally emerges. "This completes the Odyssey of the creative philosophy. With this doctrine speculation arrives at a completely 'reasonable' theory. Whitehead's God seems to be the first God of metaphysics that can really be considered personal. He is not an eternity of accomplished achievement: he is not all-powerful, nor is he all knowing as regards the future" (*Idem*, p. 150). Again he adds: "For the first time in the history of western metaphysics, God is interpreted as really anthropomorphic. For the first time, God is really the author of existence — the poet of the world. He is Plato's Demiurge, free at last from the eternity which, for centuries of speculation, seemed to deluge his efforts with determinism. Man is free because God is human" (*Idem*, p. 151).

Stallknecht's interpretation of Whitehead's conception of God corroborates what we have said. The God of Whitehead is a metaphor for the cosmic process. We can, consequently, spare ourselves the effort of pointing out how far Whitehead's conception of God is removed from the Christian doctrine of God. The fact of their mutual exclusiveness is so obvious as to need no elaboration. Whitehead says, " 'It is as true to say that God creates the World, as that the World creates God' " (p. 522). The independent self-existence of God, which is the heart of Christian teaching, is set aside completely.

It remains then to ask whether Whitehead has been able to interpret human experience so as to give it meaning. Has he been able to do more than his predecessors who have sought, in their interpretation of reality, to do without the God of Christianity? We do not think so. We may admire Whitehead's great abilities, and his great accomplishments in the field of mathematics. We may stand amazed at the ingenuity with which he has worked out his categorial scheme in *Process and Reality*. For all that, the greatest intellect will fail to find significance in cosmic happening, unless he build upon the presupposition of the self-contained God of Scripture.

Whitehead has been unable, we believe, to overcome the "bifurcation of nature" and must therefore be charged with "the fallacy of misplaced concreteness". "The final problem", he says, "is to conceive a complete fact" (*Adventures of Ideas*, p. 203; also, *Process and Reality*, pp. 27 f.). This statement comes as the climax of a long and thorough criticism of the dualism of traditional modern science. Traditional science, he argues, has put a sharp cleavage between the Observational Order and the Conceptual Order. It has worked on the assumption that it is possible to describe the Observational Order, the order of bare eventuality, without reference to the Conceptual Order. As against this he remarks, "The first point to remember is that the observational order is invariably interpreted in terms of the concepts supplied by the conceptual order" (*Adventures of Ideas*, p. 198). Or again, "Observational discrimination is not dictated by the impartial facts. It selects and discards, and what it retains is rearranged in a subjective order of prominence" (*Ibid.*). Now modern physics, he continues, has done away with the Newtonian idea of the "independent individuality of each bit of matter", with the idea of "simple location", and has substituted for it the functional inter-relationship of all things. The "thing" that we see or hear is but a "focal region" whose "influence streams away from it with finite velocity throughout the utmost recesses of space and time". "Thus the physical fact at each region of space-time is a composition of what the physical entities throughout the Universe mean for that region" (*Idem*, p. 202). A fact is not understood unless taken in its "historic route", in its functional ubiquity. It is here that Whitehead comes to the high conclusion that science needs to conceive of a complete fact.

How and where are we to look for such a complete fact? The answer is given in the immediately following sentence: "We can only form such a conception in terms of fundamental notions concerning the nature of reality" (*Idem*, p. 203). With these notions we have become acquainted. Basic to them all is the idea of pure creativity. This creativity is more fundamental than God. Whitehead makes a specific point of this when he says, "The misconception which has haunted philosophic literature throughout the centuries is the notion of 'independent existence'. There is no such mode of existence; every entity is only to be understood in terms of the way in which it is interwoven with the rest of the Universe. Unfortunately this fundamental philosophic doctrine has not been applied either to the concept of 'God', nor (in the Greek tradition) to the concept of 'Ideas'" (p. 687). In the most fundamental sense then "the Universe is open". Its "historic route" will never be finished; there is to be no far-off divine event that serves as a climax for it all. And the "historic route" of every "focal region", or of every "epochal occasion", is essentially interwoven with the "historic route" of the Universe as a whole. It is not till the Universe has run its course that a completed fact has been reached, and the Universe will never be finished. So the idea of a finished fact must always remain a "limiting concept". In practice we are left with the two orders, that of observation and that of conceptualization, unreconciled. Philosophy "seeks those generalities which characterize the complete reality of fact, and apart from which any fact must sink into an abstraction" (*Adventures of Ideas*, p. 187), while yet pure creativity by its protean character makes such generalities forever impossible of attainment. "Nothing is more impressive", says Whitehead, "than the fact that as mathematics withdrew increasingly into the upper regions of ever greater extremes of abstract thought, it returned back to earth with a corresponding growth of importance for the analysis of concrete fact" (*Science and the Modern World*, p. 48). This fact is indeed impressive, but Whitehead's philosophy offers no explanation for it. His philosophy leaves us on the one hand with "mere mathematics", and on the other hand with facts of "simple location". And, to use the author's own words, "There is no valid inference from mere possibility to matter of fact, or, in other words, from mere mathematics to concrete nature" (*Adventures of Ideas*, p. 161). The realm of abstract attributes stands unreconciled over against the realm of pure accident.

We realize that Whitehead requires no more than that science and philosophy should be on the way to truth. But how can one know that he is on the way to truth? To know that we are on the way, we must, according to Whitehead, conceive the idea of a complete fact. But his own most basic conceptions allow for no such fact. We can never know such a fact. To know such a fact would be to have the world of observation and the world of conceptualization coterminous with one another. But by definition these worlds can never be coterminous with one another. Moreover, if they were, man would be omniscient. We must know all about everything to know anything, and if we know anything we know everything. This dilemma, which has always faced the great non-Christian philosophers, faces Whitehead too.

This dilemma cannot be met, we are compelled to hold, unless we presuppose the cotermineity of the order of conceptualization and of the order of observation in the self-complete ontological trinity. It is upon this presupposition alone, we contend, that the "fallacy of misplaced concreteness" can be avoided. If we make the "bifurcation of nature" extend, as Whitehead wants it to extend, to the being of God, we have no right to expect a "philosophy of organism" to come out of the crucible of our thought. Unless God is placed back of creativity, mere mathematics or bare attributes, on the one hand, and pure accidents or brute facts, on the other hand, will stand in ultimate antagonism over against one another. There is for Whitehead's doctrine a "mysterious reality in the background, intrinsically unknowable by any direct intercourse". He declines to follow Bergson in seeking contact with the world of observation by direct intuition as such. He realizes that "substantial thing cannot call unto substantial thing" (*Idem*, p. 170). He therefore seeks for "explanatory description" similar in nature to the *Wesensschau* of certain recent German philosophers. But much as we appreciate the criticism he offers of the sharp separation between a world of description and a world of explanation, we cannot grant that his own "explanatory description" has overcome the dualism he is so anxious to escape. There is no escape from this dualism, if we begin with dualism. The "third man" difficulty may be urged against Whitehead as it has historically been urged against Plato. Plato's Demiurge was unable to bridge the gulf between the world of Ideas and the world of sense; it constituted nothing more than a concession to mythology. Whitehead's God is unable to bridge the gulf between his world of "eternal objects" and the world of "epochal occasions"; he, too, is nothing more than metaphor and illustration. Symbolising the idea of power, he is powerless still.

Whitehead's philosophy, we believe, makes extremely valuable reading. And the present volume helps us greatly to obtain a unified picture of that philosophy. Like Dewey's philosophy, it seeks to be truly consistent in the thoroughness with which it applies the process idea. As such it may help believing scholars to rely no longer upon the sharp separation between the supposedly innocent "descriptions" and the dangerous "explanations" of a non-Christian science. Whitehead shows clearly that every description involves explanation. Though not always consistent on this point, his main criticism of traditional science is to that effect. It is therefore up to those who hold to Christianity to show that true scientific description or interpretation and true philosophic generalisation can be undertaken upon Christian presuppositions only. This is not to say that non-Christian scientists do not give much true description; they undoubtedly do; but they do this with borrowed capital; they do this on the basis of the "complete fact" which is the God of Scripture. This is the God

whom they ignorantly worship; this is the God whom we know by grace
and would therefore preach unto men as the One without whom no aspect
of life has meaning, and with whom all aspects of life have meaning.

Reinhold Niebuhr: *The Nature and Destiny of Man: A Christian Interpretation.* II — *Human Destiny.* Charles Scribner's Sons. 1943. xiii, 329.
$2.75.

As in the first volume of his Gifford Lectures Professor Niebuhr dealt
primarily with human nature, so in the second he deals primarily with
human destiny. The two together offer a comprehensive philosophy of
history. This subject stands in the forefront of theological and philosophical discussion today. The mere mention of such works as *The Interpretation
of History* by Paul Tillich, *The Meaning of History* by Nicolas Berdyaev,
Time and Eternity in Christian Thought by F. H. Brabant and *Philosophy
& History, Essays presented to Ernst Cassirer,* is enough to indicate this
fact. Generally speaking the recent works dealing with the philosophy
of history presuppose a critical epistemology. Such is also the case with
the work before us. More particularly it is Kierkegaard's notion of the
Individual, as having true particularity and true universality within itself,
that has captivated Niebuhr's mind. But Niebuhr is the slave of none.
His work merits attention on its own account. In the American scene it
presents a challenge to liberalism and orthodoxy alike.

Like so many modern works on the philosophy of history the present
volume wants to make it very clear that it is anti-metaphysical. We are
to have no truck with what Hegel called the *alte Metaphysik.* Once and
for all we have done with the *thing in itself.* We simply deal with natural
experience and its rational analysis (p. 96). There may, and even must,
be that which is beyond human experience, but a beyond that is self-
contained would be irrelevant to us. The only God we can allow for is one
that stands in dialectical relationship to us. Applied to the general idea of
history this means what Niebuhr says in such passages as the following:
"The significance of the affirmation that God is revealed in Christ, and
more particularly in his Cross, is that the love (*agape*) of God is conceived
in terms which make the divine involvement in history a consequence of
precisely the divine transcendence over the structures of history" (p. 71).
It is only this sort of God that answers to the true idea of man. Each man
is an individual. As such he is both involved in and transcendent over the

historical process (p. 36). "Man is, and yet is not, involved in the flux of nature and time. He is a creature, subject to nature's necessities and limitations; but he is also a free spirit who knows of the brevity of his years and by this knowledge transcends the temporal by some capacity within himself" (p. 1). A God wholly above history, one not himself naturally involved in history, could be of no service to man. It is only if both God and man are alike involved in and alike above history that they can stand in relationship with one another. And the relation between them may then be said to be dialectical in character.

The nature of the dialectical relationship between God and man appears more fully in what is said about the person of Christ. The Christ also must be beyond, but not too absolutely beyond, man. Man has need of one who is more supra-natural than he is himself. Any particular man is too tightly bound to nature. No individual has become anything like what he may be. But a Christ who is wholly supra-natural would be useless to man. The Christ must be paradoxically related to man. The church sought to give expression to this paradoxical relationship in the Chalcedon creed. But "by stating this double facet of Christ in ontic terms, a truth of faith, which can be expressed only symbolically, is transmuted into a truth of speculative reason" (p. 60). The result was "logical nonsense". "But", says Niebuhr, "the logical nonsense is not as serious a defect as the fact that the statement tends to reduce Christian faith to metaphysical truths which need not be apprehended inwardly by faith" (p. 61). The orthodox doctrine would establish man in his "false security and pride".

What has been said so far may suffice to indicate briefly the metaphysics of Niebuhr's book. To be anti-metaphysical in the post-Kantian sense of the term means to have a metaphysics of correlativity between God and man. The first great theologian to define Christianity in terms of this correlativism was Schleiermacher. The essence of Christianity, argues Schleiermacher in effect, can be set aside only if we spoil the dialectical tension between God and man. This may be done in either of two ways. We may lift man up so high and bring the Christ down so low as virtually to identify them. Or we may push man down so low and lift the Christ up so high as to break all contact between them. A speculative theology always tends to either one or the other of them; it is only if we are anti-metaphysical, it is only if we think of dogmas as faith-constructs that we can maintain the true essence of Christianity (*The Christian Faith*, Engl. tr., pp. 94 ff.). Niebuhr has not materially altered the basic contention of Schleiermacher. When he argues that the Greeks did not expect the Christ and the Jews expected the wrong Christ, he is virtually saying what

Schleiermacher said. The Greeks, says Niebuhr, want to save man by taking him out of history, while the Jews want to bring salvation down to something that takes place directly within history. The former maintain that man is not really man till he is wholly supra-historical and the latter contend that true manhood can be fully expressed in history. The truth, he reasons, lies in between. Man must be saved both by fulfillment in, and by liberation from, history. History must not be swallowed up in eternity and eternity must not be swallowed up in history. The perfect Individual, the one who realizes the true idea of manhood as our ideal, must, as it were, be wholly above and wholly within history. It is the "second Adam" that meets these requirements.

The anti-metaphysical metaphysics of Niebuhr is, we note, supposed to do at least these two things: (1) it is to save the essence of Christianity and (2) it is to save us from the "logical nonsense" of orthodoxy. These two are, for Niebuhr, involved in one another. This is strikingly illustrated in what he says about the wrath and the mercy of God. The two, he contends, must be taken as dialectically involved in one another. If not so taken we destroy them both and at the same time return to the "logical nonsense" of orthodoxy. Wrath is not an attitude of displeasure by some God who is wholly eternal, towards man who is wholly temporal. On the contrary wrath is an aspect of the structure of a Reality that has both an eternal and a temporal aspect. "The wrath of God is the world in its essential structure reacting against the sinful corruptions of that structure; it is the law of life as love, which the egotism of man defies, a defiance which leads to the destruction of life" (p. 56). And mercy as expressed in the idea of atonement is not the act of a God who can do what he pleases inasmuch as he is sovereign over the universe. Mercy, too, is a part of the structure of the Universe that is inclusive of both God and man. "The revelation of the Atonement is precisely a 'final' word because it discloses a transcendent divine mercy which represents the 'freedom' of God in quintessential terms: namely God's freedom over His own law. Yet this freedom is not capricious. It is paradoxically related to God's law, to the structure of the world. This is the paradox of the Atonement, of the revelation of the mercy of God in its relation to the justice of God" (p. 67). It is always the Universe or Reality that is Niebuhr's final subject of predication. This Reality is full of tensions, the most fundamental of all being that of time and eternity. Involved in this basic tension of time and eternity is that of wrath and mercy. Man will always be temporal and as such always under the wrath of God. Man will always be eternal and thus always under the mercy of God. The sin and grace antithesis is inherent in the time-eternity antithesis; ethics and metaphysics are at bottom one.

In all this we have Niebuhr's equivalent to what Tillich calls the "dimension of depth" in human experience. By means of it we are to escape the flat moralism of modern liberal theology. Having no truly dialectical conception of sin, liberalism, Niebuhr argues, has an inadequate notion of the mercy of God. Niebuhr would call liberalism back to a deeper sense of sin and a deeper sense of the grace of God. He presents a challenge to many of his contemporaries on this point. Yet it is orthodoxy rather than liberalism that is his chief foe. The basic contrast running through the whole book is that between "literalism" and dialecticism. Liberalism may lack for depth of insight into the wrath and mercy of God; it is not logically nonsensical nor as such destructive of Christianity itself as orthodoxy is. We do well then to bring out more fully the contrast between dialecticism and literalism or orthodoxy as Niebuhr sees it. This will enable us to understand more clearly the general principles so far discussed.

To begin with, literalism requires us to believe in an actual state of historical perfection at the beginning of history. But this is nonsensical. Such a state cannot have existed. History is in the nature of the case always subject to the wrath of God. Original sin is therefore more profoundly original than Calvin ever thought of making it. If we wish to use the idea of a perfect man we must always look forward to it as an ideal, but never backward to it as a reality. Life *"can approach its original innocency only by aspiring to its unlimited end"* (p. 77).

Moreover, if, *per impossible*, we imagine a perfect man at the beginning of history such a man could have had no permanent and all-determinative influence on his posterity. Every individual, though in one sense subject to nature, is also above nature. That is, every man at every point in time has a direct as well an an indirect relationship to eternity. No man is fully determined by his historical antecedents. Every man is free as Adam was free. Every man is and must be his own Adam. Thus original sin is not nearly so serious a thing as Calvin made of it. The idea of a first Adam is meaningless unless it is made subordinate to the idea of the second Adam.

But literalism spoils the idea of the second Adam as much as that of the first. As it fails to understand the symbolism of the first Adam's innocency so it also fails to understand the symbolism of the second Adam's perfection. As it brings the innocency of the first Adam down into history, so it also brings the sinlessness of the second Adam down into history. But the historical Jesus was not perfect. If he had been he would not have been historical (p. 73). Christ as the second Adam ought rather to be taken as

the essential man, "the perfect norm of human character" (p. 76). As such
he reveals to us the ideal of sacrificial love. The first Adam lived in a state
of innocence. That is, history began with natural undifferentiated life.
But as freedom developed, good and evil also developed. And evil seemed
likely to prevail over the good, for "a strategy of brotherhood which has
no other resource but historical experience degenerates from mutuality to
a prudent regard for the interests of the self . . . ." (p. 96). It is here that
the idea of the second Adam comes in. Christ stands for the idea of sacrificial love. This love can never be actually realized fully in history as such;
it must always remain primarily ideal. It "has its primary justification in
an 'essential reality' which transcends the realities of history, namely, the
character of God" (ibid.). But God, it will be remembered, stands in
paradoxical relation to man. Though transcendent above, he is also of
necessity involved in, history. Accordingly sacrificial love, while it is
always essentially an ideal above history must yet make its contact with
history. The Cross always represents a "transcendent perfection": "The
New Testament never guarantees the historical success of the 'strategy'
of the Cross" (p. 87). For this reason "it is not even right to insist that
every action of the Christian must conform to agape, rather than to the
norms of relative justice and mutual love by which life is maintained and
conflicting interests are arbitrated in history" (p. 88). Yet the Cross is not
wholly above history. As the ideal of sacrificial love it is a "desirable end
of historical striving". Jesus' perfection, then, must be thought of as genuine historical striving for the always receding and primarily supra-
historical ideal. Literalism has no eye for this.

Niebuhr's teaching on the consummation of history naturally accords
with the symbolism of the first and second Adam of which we have spoken.
And this time Jesus and Paul are among the literalists whose views must
first be discarded. "One seemingly serious, but actually superficial, change
in Jesus' own interpretation must be made. He expected the historic
interim between the first and second establishment of the Kingdom to be
short. In this error he was followed both by St. Paul and the early church,
with the consequent false and disappointed hope of the parousia in the
lifetime of the early disciples" (pp. 49 f.). There was a very good excuse
for this mistake. It was the most natural thing for people to think in
terms of years when they spoke of the relation of time to eternity. "This
error was due to an almost inevitable illusion of thought which deals with
the problem of the relation of time and eternity. The eschata which represents the fulfillment and the end of time in eternity are conceived
literally and thereby made a point in time. The sense that the final ful-

fillment impinges on the present moment, the feeling of urgency in regard to anticipating this fulfillment, expressed itself in chronological terms and thereby becomes transmuted into a 'proximate futurism,' into the feeling that the fulfillment of history is chronologically imminent" (p. 50).

Apparently neither Jesus nor Paul realized that it is "important to take Biblical symbols seriously but not literally" (*ibid.*). By taking them literally they seem to have imperilled "the dialectical relation between history and superhistory" (*ibid.*). Niebuhr speaks of Jesus' mistake as only apparently serious. Yet when others make the same mistake that Jesus is said to have made, it is said to be destructive of Christianity and logically nonsensical. What Niebuhr is really saying is that the historical Jesus was quite mistaken in his basic philosophy of history. For the difference between the literalism of Jesus and the dialecticism of Niebuhr is not limited to a question of earlier and later. According to Niebuhr, Jesus was simply and radically wrong in thinking that anywhere in history a state of perfection could ever exist.

Niebuhr seeks to avoid the logic of this situation by distinguishing his position from that of Albert Schweitzer. Speaking of Schweitzer's views he says: "According to his conception the whole ethic and religion of Jesus is based upon the illusion of his proximate return" (*ibid.*). Then he adds: "The real fact is that the absolute character of the ethic of Jesus conforms to the actual constitution of man and history, that is, to the transcendent freedom of man over the contingencies of nature and the necessities of time, so that only a final harmony of life with life in love can be the ultimate norm of his existence" (pp. 50 f.). But surely the palm of consistency must be accorded to Schweitzer rather than to Niebuhr. The Jesus of Niebuhr's portrait is really both radically wrong and radically right, while yet he is assumed to be essentially consistent with himself. Jesus is said to be really an expert in reading off human nature correctly. That is, Jesus is in effect to be taken as the first genuine dialecticist. He saw clearly that man is inherently both temporal and supra-natural, that history must therefore always contain both evil and good. Yet Jesus was also a literalist living under the delusion that his second coming in perfection would take place at a point in time. He was the first one really to originate the true Christ idea as always ideal and then destroyed this ideal by making of it a reality of history as such. Niebuhr has no logical right on his principles to dismiss the literalism of Jesus as a minor matter. He should at least have spoken of a serious lapse on the part of Jesus from true dialecticism into destructive literalism.

More basic that that, Niebuhr should have cut himself loose from the historical Jesus altogether. The historical Jesus took the Old Testament with its story of creation literally. He claimed to be without sin and he claimed that he would return on the clouds of heaven as his disciples had seen him go. If Niebuhr wants to hold to a dialectical construction of reality, it is well, but the legitimacy of his attributing it to the Jesus of history must be questioned.

The same point must also be made with respect to what the volume before us says about the Reformation. Niebuhr presents his dialectical reconstruction of Christianity as being truly Protestant in character. Rome, he says, had claimed to have escaped the ambiguities of history (p. 145). The Reformers, on the other hand, understood the nature of the Biblical paradox. Even so they fell back frequently into the Roman error (p. 203). They made absolute distinctions between those that were and those that were not justified by faith. In this they were mistaken. History allows of no absolute distinctions anywhere. "This fact suggests that Reformation insights must be related to the whole range of human experience more 'dialectically' than the Reformation succeeded in doing. The 'yes' and 'no' of its dialectical affirmations: that the Christian is *justus et peccator*,' 'both sinner and righteous'; that history fulfills and negates the kingdom of God; that grace is continuous with, and in contradiction to, nature; that Christ is what we ought to be and also what we cannot be; that the power of God is in us and that the power of God is against us in judgment and mercy; that all these affirmations which are but varied forms of the one central paradox of the relation of the Gospel to history must be applied to the experiences of life from top to bottom" (p. 204). Here, too, it would have been better if Niebuhr had set his position fully and frankly in opposition to that of the Reformers. Luther and Calvin were anything but paradoxical in the main thrust of their theology. They were followers of Jesus and Paul in their literalism. Luther and Calvin thought history was a fit medium for the direct expression of the plan of God; indeed they thought of history as being nothing other than an expression of that plan. The idea of an ideal limit always suprahistorical as well as historical, such as a "critically informed" modern theology offers us, was foreign to their thought. The "new synthesis" that, according to Niebuhr, is the need of the hour, ought therefore to have been presented as wholly new, or at least as being as new as *The Critique of Pure Reason*.

If the dialecticism of Niebuhr is calculated to save the essence of Christianity, it is so because it is at the same time calculated to destroy historic Christianity. Such has been the conclusion of what has been said up to this point. A life and death struggle will naturally ensue between those who still hold to historical Christianity and those who follow the "new synthesis" that is offered by Niebuhr's dialecticism. Niebuhr claims that literalism or orthodoxy has given us a false reading of human nature and history. This claim has not been substantiated in his book. Indeed the charge that he makes on this score with respect to orthodoxy must be made with respect to himself.

For Niebuhr there are two orders of reality. The one consists of the contingencies of nature and the necessities of time. The other is that of timeless rationality or logic. The one is called natural and the other supranatural or rational. And man is said to participate in both. He warns us not to forget this fact. Man must not be taken as belonging to the natural order only. Nor must he be taken as belonging to the rational order only. We must not be naturalists. Nor must we be rationalists. We must be dialecticists. Naturalism misreads and destroys experience. Rationalism does the same. But by joining naturalism and rationalism we read experience aright and save the meaning of history. Such is, broadly speaking, the nature of the argument of the present, as of the previous, volume. But why the adding of two errors should produce the truth is not apparent.

The defenders of Niebuhr's position will no doubt exclaim that dialecticism is not the mere addition of naturalism and rationalism. Is not the whole more than its parts? Does not the whole even precede its parts? When naturalism and rationalism are made correlative to one another in dialecticism they have lost their identity, they have become quite different in character.

To this we would make the following reply. It cannot be shown that in dialecticism the whole is greater than its parts. Dialecticism is not a unity that controls its parts. It is but a dictatorial cohesion by which rationalism and naturalism are brought together against their will. This is apparent from the fact that Niebuhr is, throughout his book, either a rationalist or a naturalist. It is only the rapidity with which he shifts from one position to the other that gives the appearance of something else.

We are told that dialecticism is simply the correct reading of experience. Yet the nature of experience is basically determined by purely rationalist methods. Niebuhr simply swings about the law of non-contradiction to determine what is possible and impossible. The existence of a transcendent God above history is said to be impossible, and why? Because such existence would not be penetrable to the intellect of man. The idea of an originally perfect man is said to be impossible, and why? Again because it is not penetrable to the intellect of man. The Chalcedon creed is said to present us with logical nonsense, and why? It, too, is not penetrable to the intellect of man. The idea of a final victory over evil in history is said to be impossible, and why? Again because it is not penetrable to the mind of man. Thus the intellect is sent out to bring down the mountains and lift up the valleys in John the Baptist fashion in preparation for the coming of experience. All reality has been swept clean of that which might have qualities of its own and thus prove to be in any measure determinative of experience. Experience may now be truly free and unrestrained. Or, so it seems.

When the intellect has swept all things clean it has at the same time prescribed strict limits for experience. John the Baptist has claimed to be the Messiah himself. Experience that has accepted the services of rationalism for purposes of clearance is bound to trade with rationalism when it seeks for positive content. And this is the death of experience as anything that is intelligible. It means that experience to have meaning must become pure formal logic. To have meaning, experience must become timeless. For individuals to have relations with other individuals they must all become universals. For Frenchmen to be Frenchmen and for Poles to be Poles they must become members of the *Reich*.

Of course experience may seek to escape its own destruction at the hands of Master Intellect by refusing to trade with him at all. But then it must be sub-rational or non-rational. The individual to be a true individual must then have no contact with any other individual. Every Frenchman not ready to be a true Frenchman and every Pole not ready to be a true Pole by leaving home for work in a munitions factory of the *Reich* may make a fox-hole for himself at home and remain there the rest of his natural life. That is to say the "contingencies of nature" of which Niebuhr speaks are what they are in their utter meaninglessness just because his world of meaning is a world of abstract logic. Naturalism and rationalism are always close friends.

The dialecticism of Niebuhr now appears for what it really is. Niebuhr is first a rationalist. The logic of his rationalism would lead him to the position of Parmenides. Unwilling to land there, he assumes the ultimacy of change. But the change he thus assumes must be irrational. If it is not irrational it is, on his basis, not change. So Niebuhr is secondly a naturalist. But unwilling to be either a rationalist or a naturalist he stands with one foot on one and with one foot on the other position, apparently hoping thus to make a fine-pulling team of them. But pure rationalism and pure irrationalism each want to control everything. Each horse will pull in the opposite direction from the other for all it is worth. Dialecticism is but the attempt to ride off with both horses in opposite directions at the same time.

This is not to say that dialecticism is any less acceptable than either outright rationalism or outright naturalism. It is only to say that, when the presuppositions of historic Christianity are left behind, human experience and history must be read in terms of abstractly rationalistic or abstractly naturalistic categories. Niebuhr's Gifford Lectures are a work of great learning and ingenuity, but they cannot conceal this fact. When a great theologian, dexterously handling the tools the great logicians of modern times have given him and fully conversant with the literature of methodology, seeks ever so hard to unite rationalism and naturalism in such a way as to produce something new and fails to do so, then it is fresh cause for encouragement to those who have ever held that the historic Christian faith alone gives the true reading of experience and the true meaning to history. Historic Christianity presupposes a self-sufficient God in whom eternal meaning is eternal activity. This God is, to be sure, not penetrable by the mind of man. For this very reason, however, it is possible to avoid the fatal error of naturalism. Because historic Christianity is not rationalistic it need not be naturalistic. It is only because God's counsel is inscrutable to man that it is wide enough and basic enough to include "whatsoever comes to pass". Only a logic than is higher than, and prior to, that of man can provide for genuine individuality, genuine meaning and genuine progress in human experience. Only a logic that is higher than, and basic to, that of man can provide for facts a meaning that is not destructive of those very facts. It is only because historic Christianity is supra-rational and supra-natural that it is not absurd. *Credo quia non absurdum est.*

28

C. E. M. Joad: *God and Evil*. New York: Harper & Brothers. 1943. 349. $3.00.

On the jacket of Dr. Joad's book we read the following words: "England's great philosopher, formerly an agnostic, tells how present world events have brought him to a new belief in God". We shall briefly consider what these words may mean in the light of what Joad says.

An interesting aubiographical note runs through Joad's book. The names of Aldous Huxley, H. G. Wells, Bertrand Russell and C. E. M. Joad, he says, "have come to sound like an incantation which the priest murmurs as with bell, book and candle he adjures the people to turn their backs on the dark river of thought and return to the lighted way of simple faith" (p. 281). The implication is that, of course, there has never been any justification for such an unseemly attitude. For "the fundamental truths of religion do not seem to fall into the self-evident class; if they did, there would not be so much disagreement as to what they are, or so much doubt as to whether they are true" (pp. 25 f.).

Joad is careful to enumerate the various difficulties connected with the "religious hypothesis". He says: "The evidence for God is far from plain. The evidence for a good God is in the highest degree dubious; so at least, I have always believed . . . . . . If it be said that the universe must have a cause, since it could not have arisen from nothing, and that God was the cause, the question arises why does not the same consideration apply in the case of God? Must he too not have had a cause? . . . . . . One might, that is to say, just as well begin with a mysterious universe, *there* from the first, as with a mysterious God *there* from the first" (p. 59). And it may well be doubted whether such objections have ever been answered (p. 61).

Why then re-open the question? Well, because of "the obtrusiveness of evil". With such modern theologians as Reinhold Niebuhr and others, Joad has learned to conclude "that what the religions have always taught is true, and that evil is endemic in the heart of man" (p. 20). The universe is not running "according to plan". With Stephen Vincent Benét's new settlers in Virginia, Joad seems, as it were, to say:

"We die, we die!
There are seven dead in four days — and every morning
We drag them out of their cabins like stiffened dogs
To lie in the hateful earth of this wilderness
Where we thought to find the gold".

The forest-god is "sleepily vexed" at last, weaving round us with the vapors of a deadly marsh. And when we fire into the forest of pure possibility with the muskets of rational arrangement there is nothing. It verily daunts a man. To use Joad's own words: "To be confronted with a universe which contains evil as an ultimate and ineradicable fact, to know that there is no defence against it save in the strength or rather in the weakness of one's own character, no hope of overcoming it save through the efficacy of one's own unaided efforts — *this* I find to be a position almost intolerably distressing" (pp. 103 f.). Joad accordingly wants to make use of "the grace of God" (p. 104) if it is really available to man. But is it? How do we find out? What must be our method?

The method is, of course, that of experience. As a true Quartermaster-General, Joad calls the men of "first ascents", the experts on tropical and arctic weather. We must learn to fight not only in Maine in summer and in Florida in winter, we must also prepare to enter the jungle with its malaria and the arctic with its deadly frost and wind. So we make our experiments in Washington, D. C. We consult our "table of basic allowances" and send our men into the cold chamber where it is 60° below zero or into our simulated desert with the thermometer at 120° and a hot wind blowing sand in their faces.

That is to say, Joad does not pretend that his rôle as the returned prodigal is to be taken as anything more than a rôle. There is to be no place for any sort of revelation on the part of the God in which he is to believe. We have enough information about the various climatic conditions of the world to enable us to prepare in Washington, D. C., by our own laboratories, for the worst of evils that can befall us. The world has been pretty well explored from the south pole to the north. Our "pile garments", our dehydrated and compressed K rations will enable our soldiers to meet and conquer the enemy anywhere. We shall insist that the Indians "stand in battalia to be butchered" rather than slip from tree to tree. We shall make muskets that make more noise than the old ones we had at the beginning of the war. If Christianity comes to us with the claim to be for all men, says Joad, we shall concede the claim. But this "concession carries with it the right of all men freely to examine and, if they be so minded, to reject the pretensions of the claimant". (p. 280).

In his last chapter Joad lays down in detail some of the things the Indians are not to be permitted to do. They must never go beyond the reach of our muskets or the sight of our eyes. The God he wants to believe in is not to be one who determines all things by His plan. There is to be no creation out of nothing, or of man in the image of God. There is, too, no unique claim to be made for Jesus as though He were in any unique sense the Son of God and as though anything that He did in Palestine at a certain date in history had any particular significance. "Is it really conceivable that our descendants a hundred million years hence will still be looking back to this event as unique and central in the history of the planet? Credible even that our descendants ten million years hence should so regard it?" (p. 295). A million Frenchmen cannot be wrong. Then, too, there is to be no exclusion of any one from the "grace of God". Speaking of Socrates and Plato, Joad says: "As to the exclusive claim to salvation, the claim that believing Christians will pass their eternal life in more desirable circumstances, at a higher moral level, and with greater spiritual enlightenment than these men, I do not see how it can be either proved or disproved. I content myself with the remark that a universe in which such a claim was true would seem to me to be a non-moral universe, and the God who prescribed the law which made the claim true, an unjust God" (p. 298). In fact any one who turns to the gospel narrative will find nothing very attractive in Jesus. Many of his utterances are really meaningless. There are many inconsistencies in what he says. He "makes assertions that have been shown to be untrue . . . . . But it is the character of Jesus Himself that I found most disconcerting. I was astonished at the lack of warrant for the 'gentle Jesus, meek and mild' conception in which I had been nurtured" (p. 104). Jesus is "touchily sensitive and liable to break out into torrents of denunciation on what seems to me very inadequate provocation" (*ibid.*). He dislikes being "asked for evidence". He equates sin with "an inability to assent to what must have seemed highly dubious propositions" (p. 305). Most disturbing of all is the "anti-intellectual bias" of Jesus. "He abuses men of learning, denounces the critical attitude in order to throw into favourable relief that of unquestioning acceptance, and tells people that it is only if they become as little children, and, therefore, as innocent and, presumably, as ignorant as little children, that they can hope to understand Him and be saved" (p. 307).

In short, the God of orthodox Christianity is no more acceptable to Joad now than He has ever been. Any hostility that he may formerly have had against religion, says Joad, has long since disappeared (p. 281), and adds "I would like to believe, even if I cannot" (*ibid.*). But as for historic Christianity and its God, well, that is something else. Speaking of orthodox Christians he says: "Why should I be frightened of provoking those who have never been my friends?" (*ibid.*), and adds: "I too have my prides and vanities, and one of them is to follow reason wherever it leads" (*ibid.*). And on Joad's premises following reason amounts to denying God.

There is no point, then, in Joad's saying that he has met the orthodox half way (*ibid.*). He has in this work as much as in any earlier work done everything he can to make their faith appear irrational and immoral. One who follows reason and the facts of science, and one who follows the moral sense that he has within him, Joad argues, must reject the claim of historic Christianity throughout.

Nor is there any point in Joad's saying that "the heart demands, even if the reason still denies" (*ibid.*), for the demands of his reason and his heart are in perfect accord with one another. His heart condemns as unjust a universe in which things do not happen according to plan, that is the plan of human reason, and his reason limits the field of possibility so that nothing can happen that will seem unjust to what he thinks are the legitimate claims of his heart. Oppressed with the reality of evil, arguing vigorously against the subjectivist or idealist and oriental evaporation of its objectivity, he takes pains not to define evil and sin in relation to the God of Christianity. Evil is still to be defined in terms of man and his own self-sufficient ideals of morality. Lying prostrate in his cabin with malaria, the poison arrows of the darkwood Indians killing on every side, helpless without the "grace of God",

"There came the savages, smiling, bringing corn,
. . . .
As if compelled by something past all plans,
Some old, barbaric courtesy of man's,
Wild as his heart, red as his hunter's dreams
— And for no cause the white men ever knew".

Somehow, somehow, no one knows how, the Ethiopian will change his own skin and the leopard by licking himself diligently or by applying Rid-o Spot, a "fabric cleaner that's different, Safer and Better" but manufactured by the well-known firm of Goulard & Olena, Inc., 140 Liberty Street, New York, N. Y., will change his spots. Man finds the grace of God within and no wonder, for man himself is God.

To return now to the statement quoted from the jacket of the book, near the end of his work Joad says that as a returning prodigal he is "only just on the affirmative side of agnosticism" (p. 278). In reality he is more sure than ever now that God does not exist. All he has contended for is that there is hidden in human personality something more than the historical materialists and subjectivists have been willing to concede. The "little clearings" of science are "small in the forest". We have just landed in

Virginia. Unexpectedly the "hazel arrows" rain thick from the coverts, and the Indian yell goes up. Never fear, for possibility itself lies no further west than the Pacific ocean. Daunted for the moment our brilliant Quartermaster staff will write off the "impossibles" as they come and teach us to hunt and trap all the evils that are "endemic to the human heart". There is no God; we are not creatures of God, we are not sinners before God, we need no salvation through Christ, but all of us will be saved by the grace of ourselves and of the universe that, we and our millions of posterity insist, shall be moral.

Joad says he has been impressed "by the obtrusiveness of evil"; we reply that he has not even seen the first glimpse of the true nature of evil. Virtually denying the existence of God, he has also virtually denied the existence of evil. How can there be evil in distinction from good, how can there be meaning in the terms better and worse, if reality is what Joad says or assumes that it is? On his basis all that is is good or, it may as well be said, all that is is evil. Rejecting the fall of man as an historical fact, Joad to all intents and purposes thinks of evil as part of the ultimate metaphysical situation. Why then, Plato would argue, dare we hope that the ideas of "mud and hair and filth" will not be as permanent as the ideas of the true, the good and the beautiful? As a realist, Joad has no answer to the subjectivist. As a dualist, Joad has no answer to the monist. All that because, on his assumption of man's ultimacy, he places reason in the midst of pure or bare possibility. If evil is what his metaphysics virtually asserts it is, namely, pure uncontrolled factuality, it should, like the Virginia swamp of Benét's poem, make all the white carpenters and bricklayers from merry England "purge out their entrails" and disappear forever. On the other hand, if evil is, what his epistemology says it must be, fully reachable by the musketry of reason set on the emplacement of autonomous man, one fine sweeping dictatorial purge will remove all Indians and mosquitoes as well.

It is, of course, not for lack of intellectual acumen that Joad has been unable even to present the issues clearly, let alone offer any solution for the problem of evil. As one of the most brilliant and most popular writers on philosophy in our day, Joad cannot even state the basic problem of philosophy because that problem can be stated only in terms of the God who by his assumption is excluded from his view.

REVIEWS OF BOOKS

ed. Dagobert D. Runes: *Twentieth Century Philosophy.* New York: Philosophical Library. 1943. 571. $5.00.

There are in the volume before us some twenty essays by as many outstanding men in the field of philosophy. Each of these essays merits separate discussion. As this is not feasible we limit ourselves to a few observations that are of special interest to those who hold to historic Christianity. The claim has frequently been made that both recent philosophy and recent science are favorably disposed to the "values" of Christianity. It will be our concern to inquire what measure of justification there is for such a claim in the essays of *Twentieth Century Philosophy.*

The writers of the present volume are as a whole anxious to incorporate the results of recent scientific developments into their philosophical pictures. But there is, quite naturally, some difference of opinion as to the import of the latest scientific pronouncements. The main point in dispute seems to be whether an idealist or a realist conclusion is to be drawn from the work of such men as Planck, Heisenberg and Einstein. This point may be briefly illustrated as follows.

As in his recent book on *The Survival of Western Culture* so in the essay included in the present volume Ralph T. Flewelling makes the most of recent scientific views as evidence for the legitimacy of the personalist point of view in philosophy. Speaking of the changes in the scientific outlook he says: "In the course of about thirty years we have advanced from the affirmation that the most certain of all realities is the atom (made by Lord Kelvin) to the contrary affirmation that the most certain of all certainties is the principle of uncertainty. In all the history of philosophic and scientific thought the world has not been faced by so complete and so significant a reversal of opinion since the days of Copernicus" (p. 335). A little later he adds: "Reality can no longer be conceived as something 'out there' in which the person has no part nor lot. What is 'out there' is also a function of what is 'in here' and can be understood only by reference to it" (*ibid.*). So then, Flewelling argues in his book and suggests in the article, the last great obstacle to the glorious onward march of human personality has been removed.

"But", says Victor F. Lenzen, as if in reply to Flewelling, "the idealist interpretation of relativity is not necessary. The relativity of space, time and other quantities to the observer is, precisely expressed, with respect to physical frames of reference, so that observers using the same frame would find the same values of particular quantities, except for errors of observation. Furthermore, the theory of relativity has introduced the concept of absolute space-time with properties common to all observers. Events in space-time may be viewed as independent of mind as well as dependent" (pp. 122 f.).

Perhaps the most representative point of view on the philosophic import of the latest scientific picture is expressed by Bertrand Russell. As Lenzen contends that the idealist and the realist may find equal justification for their outlook Russell argues that the whole dispute between idealism and realism has really been shown to be meaningless. He says:

"Modern physics enables us to give body to the suggestion of Mach and James, that the 'stuff' of the *mental* and *physical* worlds is the *same*. 'Solid matter' was obviously very different from thoughts and also from the persistent ego. But if matter and the ego are both only convenient aggregations of *events*, it is much less difficult to imagine them composed out of the same materials. Moreover what has hitherto seemed one of the most marked peculiarities of mind, namely *subjectivity*, or the possession of a point of view, has now invaded physics, and is found not to involve mind: a photographic camera has it to precisely the same extent . . . . Thus physics and psychology have approached each other, and the old dualism of mind and matter has broken down" (pp. 247 f.).

The significant thing in all this would seem to be that both idealism and realism have changed so much, and in their change have come so nearly to resemble one another, that each may, almost with equal justice, claim the sympathy of the present reigning scientific point of view. The differences between the various philosophical schools as represented in the book under consideration are largely differences of names. As a common Modernism has been in many churches the means of reconciliation between Methodists, Baptists and Presbyterians, so the common desire to incorporate the latest scientific picture has made realists and idealists of various shades embrace one another. But perhaps this is to overstate the case. Perhaps we should say that the new scientific outlook is merely the occasion for a new amalgam in philosophy. The older "out there" realism and the older "in here" idealism have been out of date since the time of Kant. A new subject and a new object, less antagonistic to one another than their respective forbears were to each other, have been maturing since 1781. A. C. Ewing writing his essay on Kantianism says:

"That all propositions are partly *a priori* and partly empirical, that the mind exercises a far greater organizing function even in sense-perception than had been realized hitherto so that perception is impossible without conception and we are acquainted with nothing which is merely given without interpretation, that the unity of the self is not that of an unchanging, simple substance but is to be found in the functional unity of its experience, that the knowing self and its objects are correlative so that there can be no self without objects and no objects without an experiencing self, that physical objects are best regarded as systems of sense-data unified by the general laws common to all human experience, are doctrines which, whether right or wrong, clearly emerge from the transcendental deduction and which have exercised a great influence ever since" (p. 262).

The recent scientific revolution, then, has not really been so basic as Flewelling makes it out to be. It has merely hastened the process already inherent in the critical philosophy of Kant. If Flewelling speaks loudly of the victories of a new subjectivism, others speak loudly and with equal justice of the victories of a new objectivism. Meanwhile what is really forming is a new form of phenomenalism, a new stress on the correlativity of subject and object.

As already suggested the new Phenomenalism seeks to conserve the "virtues" of both the subjectivists and the objectivists, of the tender-minded and the tough-minded. The "spiritual values" of the personalist and the solid values of the dialectical materialist are alike to be given place in the order that is or is to be the philosophy of our day. Both Jacques Maritain and Bertrand Russell speak with feeling of the new synthesis of "essence" and "existence" in which Rome and Columbia are to have equal part.

The new conjunction of forces presupposes an old disjunction. Both the subjectivists and the objectivists are in hearty agreement that no one is ever to be molested with the old orthodox notions of the creation and the fall of man. Kant's chief influence on current philosophy is said to lie in his rejection of the old metaphysics (p. 262). This point is so generally taken for granted that it is scarcely mentioned. The various schools of philosophy represented in the present work have so completely rejected the God of historic Christianity that they simply ignore Him altogether.

Both the new subject and the new object or the new subject-object is assumed to be non-created and autonomous.

This basic disjunction is, of course, not the distinguishing mark of the new union movement. Modern philosophy has, since Kant, taken this pretty much for granted. The distinguishing feature of the new Phenomenalism would seem to lie in the consistency with which this basic disjunction is applied as a remedial measure for the removal of internal quarrels.

The older objectivism, attributing a measure of "out-thereness" to the macrocosmos, appeared to the older subjectivism as still retaining something of the older metaphysics. The older subjectivist or idealist was looking for an ultimate environment that should offer no obstruction of any sort to the free movement of his spirit. The idea of a universe controlled even in detail by the plan of God was, for the older subjectivist, the worst possible obstruction to the free activity of human personality. Now all is clear. Not even the remnants of such a position as is found in naive realism stand in the way. *The Story of American Realism*, as told by William P. Montague, shows how neo-realism and critical realism in turn have sought to remove that objection. And if their positions left anything to be desired from the subjectivist point of view the newest of new realisms assures the new subjectivists that "subjectivity" is found even in physics. The objective world has therewith become wholly pliable to the wants and needs of the subjectivist.

The older subjectivism, on the other hand, attributing a measure of "in-hereness" to the microcosmos, appeared to the older objectivism as still retaining something of the older metaphysic. The older objectivist was looking for a universe that should be wholly open for inspection and therefore exhaustively interpretable to the mind of man. The idea of a God, who exists as self-sufficient and therefore as inherently incomprehensible to the mind of man, was for the older objectivist the greatest possible obstruction for the free progress of science and philosophy. Now all is clear. Not even the remnants of such a position as that found in naive or Berkeleian subjectivism stand in the way. Was not St. Thomas really "the most *existential* of the philosophers"? Maritain assures us that he was (p. 295). Maritain wants to sit in on the new synthesis. To do so he assures his colleagues that he, too, has taken to heart the Kantian dictum that there is no subject except as correlative to its object. With Aristotle as with St. Thomas, Maritain seeks in this manner to "save the universal". The whole subjective world, that of God as well as that of man, has therewith been opened up in full fairness to every one and true objectivity maintained. As William James complained of Idealism so God may well complain of the new Phenomenalism that it does not allow Him to maintain a private bedroom for Himself.

A really fine bargain has thus been made. The objectivist is to refrain from casting nostalgic glances not only at such things as objective miracles, but even at such things as a general providence of God. The subjectivist in turn is no longer to whisper not only of subjective miracles like regeneration, but not even of any kind of mind, divine or human, as closed to inspection and control. Vying with one another in their new generosity of spirit, the subjectivist and the objectivist have sacrificed the vestigial remnants of Christian theism that they found in each other's closets. Pilate and Herod have become friends again.

With this basic reconciliation effected, it is no marvel that we hear much talk of peace everywhere. Intellectualists, voluntarists and aestheticists are seen to shake hands with one another, as conjointly they sacrifice the ewe-lamb of Christian theism. The intellectualist wants comprehensive system; he shall be satisfied; no fact shall hereafter be called a fact unless it fit into the system of the intellectualist. We shall assign to the *logical* empiricist the task of determining by means of his principles of coherence what is possible and what is not possible. Above all the God of Christianity is not to molest him by presenting to him such facts as depend for their final meaning upon His counsel. Such principles as non-contradiction are to be regarded as "negative conditions of possible being" (p. 362). The voluntarist is the man who speaks of the will, or the right, to believe. For him the test of truth is operational efficiency; he, too, shall be satisfied. All reality is historical. The universe is wide open. "Life is a risk" (p. 93), and "our action counts" (p. 94). The logical *empiricist* will see to it that there are no speculations about irrelevant absolutes (p. 385). Working out Kant's principles we thus have a "kind of 'realism' within 'idealism' " (p. 260). For "the actual world is an exemplification of the essential structures that have been determined" (p. 361). The aestheticist is the man of immediacy, of synoptic vision and appreciation. He cares not for deduction and he cares not for induction; he wants intuition. He, too, shall be satisfied. The phenomenological reduction "leads one back to the 'pure' consciousness of an individual knower as the starting-point for philosophy" (p. 353). The ordinary facts of space and time are "bracketed" and with Husserl we know the world "as it was in the first place" (p. 358). We deal with "essences" only and these essences are no longer, as they were with rationalists, the products of ratiocination; they are the correlatives of our vision. Thus we have reached rock bottom when "one inspects all beliefs in the light of his own pure experiences" (p. 359).

Thus all is to be peace. Kant's distinction between the theoretical and the practical can be dropped. There is a place for all methods (p. 346), but the final unity of all of them is found in the subject. The "basic method must be subjective" (p. 349). Aristotle's distinction between scientific knowledge and its object, on the one hand, and opinion and its object (*Posterior Analytics*, 88b), on the other, is replaced by expert perspective and its object. All systems are perspectives and all objects of systems are correlatives to the perspectives.

Another point of interest in this connection may be mentioned. With the disappearance of the sharp disjunctions between realism, idealism, intellectualism, voluntarism and aesthetecism goes the disappearance of the disjunction between scientific description and philosophic explanation. The genuine scientist sees the essences; he merely describes them for what they are and that is explanation. There simply is nothing more to be done. With the older metaphysics banned completely from the scene, there is no need to worry whether appearance corresponds to reality; appearance is reality and seeing of appearance is explanation of reality. It is "completeness of understanding on a descriptive basis" (p. 348) that forms the ideal of the new philosophy that sees things as they were in the beginning. "There is a good meaning of the term 'explanation' over against 'mere description.' Not only *how* things behave and events occur, but also *why* they do so, can be found out by science" (p. 397). And as for philosophy, its method is the same in principle as that of science; it is simply of a more general character. Thus we may treat theology as an empirical science.

The picture we have drawn of the amalgamation process that is going on in the schools of modern philosophy is far from encouraging to those who hold the historic Christian Faith. But if not altogether fanciful, there is a moral that needs scarcely to be mentioned. Christian people ought to face the facts as they are.

Facing the facts as they are, they will refrain from making alliances with any of the schools of philosophy. There is no school of philosophy in the current scene, whether realist or idealist, that is basically any more sympathetic to the Christian religion than any other. We do not say that the older realisms or idealisms were at bottom any better than the new. Our main contention is that if ever in the past there has been a measure of excuse for Christian thinkers in finding support for their position in the principles of current philosophic schools such excuse exists no longer. The issues are now more clearly drawn than ever and the hostility of all the schools to orthodox Christianity is now abundantly apparent.

The schools may differ among one another but the differences that they have are strictly prescribed by a common assumption. This assumption involves the virtual ascription to man of that which the Christian faith ascribes to God. A self-existent being whose counsel is His vision, whose will determines possibility — such is what orthodox Christianity finds its God to be. And that is exactly what all the schools of modern philosophy find man to be. Facts are what they are because God by His counsel makes them so — says the believing Christian; facts are what they are because man makes them so — say the schools. An event is a selection, for the Christian, ultimately made by God, for modern philosophy, ultimately made by man.

If, then, Christian believers want their faith to survive and if, not satisfied with that, they want every thought brought captive to the obedience of Christ, they must needs challenge the basic assumption of human autonomy that controls the various philosophers in all that they say. The commander of a battleship does not talk much about areas that he has in common with an enemy submarine. For it is with *events* that he deals. He therefore sends a depth charge *at first sight* of the submarine. Nor does he leave one area of the submarine unmolested. He cannot even do that. His own argument, once employed, is as it were, beyond his control. Christians, in challenging the basic assumption of modern philosophy and science, must deal with trees as well as with miracles. For if trees are what modern philosophy and science say they are, miracles cannot be what Christians say they are. "The 'field' of transcendental consciousness that is opened up by the epoché can be described in familiar terms. The transformation that is carried through is a universal one, so that no special symbolism is desirable, other than, perhaps, quotation-marks. Thus, 'tree' would stand for the intended tree, which is not posited as existent, but is merely the objectivity correlative to my awareness of it. It is the *noema* that corresponds to the cognitive activity, or the *noesis*" (p. 356). The golden rule is treated just as the tree is treated. It, too, is but the objective correlate to my awareness of it. "The golden rule has persisted through the ages, because it makes life livable" (p. 94), not because there is divine imperative in it. It is therefore only if the basic assumption of modern philosophy and science is challenged at every point that it can be effectively challenged at any point.

To challenge the basic assumption of modern philosophy and science is to point out that on its basis experience runs into hopeless confusion. The volume discussed gives ample evidence of this. The ship of modern philosophy and science is like to that of Melville's story *Billy Budd*. Wholly becalmed it goes equally fast in all directions the only movement being that of mutiny on board, which mutiny cannot even come to a successful termination for either party, the only termination possible being that of starvation for all. Rock bottom is reached, we are told, by means of the eidetic reduction, which orders us to inspect all beliefs in the light of one's own pure experience (p. 359). This is surely the rock bottom of the bottomless pit of solipsism. Forsaking God as the presupposition of true interpretation in any field leads to pure inactivity. Every criterion of distinction between fact and fiction, between truth and falsehood, between right and wrong, has been thrown overboard as ballast and the ship of science and philosophy is doomed to arrive at the Enchanted Islands.

There would seem to be urgent need, then, for Christian colleges to develop their philosophy and science departments and to work out their own basic methodology in distinction to that which is current round about them. A self-conscious Christian methodology in every branch of learning is the crying need of the hour.

To expect any help in the construction of such a method from Rome, would be to rely on the staff of Egypt which will be sure to pierce one's hand. Rome's philosophy is basically as humanistically oriented as that of any other school. Rome boasts of this fact. Maritain wants, following St. Thomas, to understand everything "in the light and generosity of existence" (p. 302). And at the heart of existence, we are told, St. Thomas reconciled "the intellect and mystery" (p. 299). A vague existence beyond God and man, yet open to the intellect of man — that is Rome's philosophy; that, too, is the phenomenalism a-forming before our eyes. Rome is again up to date; Rome is also aboard the good ship heading for the everlasting calms. A truly Protestant philosophy of methodology must build alone.

This is not to assert that no use whatever can be made of the description or explanation of the schools. Speaking for the dialectical materialists and setting forth their criticism of idealists John Somerville says: "It seems to the dialectical materialist that these people are 'standing on their heads,' which is an eccentric posture, but one that is not necessarily incompatible with a good deal of valuable reporting, if only the report be turned right side up" (p. 487). We may apply this to modern philosophy and science. God's created universe is so manifestly a revelation of God Himself that even those who stand on their heads, attributing to themselves the place that belongs to God, cannot help displaying, in spite of themselves, a good deal of the truth as it actually is.

Ralph Tyler Flewelling: *The Survival of Western Culture*. New York and London: Harper & Brothers. 1943. xv, 304. $3.00.

A number of years ago there appeared a book that has become famous and influential. The book was Oswald Spengler's *The Decline of the West*. Spengler argued with great learning that western civilization was doomed. Civilizations move like the hogs in a packing-house; they grunt with satisfaction for a while in their prosperity and then scream in great distress as they are turned up by the wheel of time and hung head down in line with those that have gone before.

Dr. Ralph Tyler Flewelling, Director of the School of Philosophy at the University of Southern California, does not like this lugubrious picture of the great prophet of despair. Looking at western culture afresh, he thinks it is time now for optimism. The new scientific developments and the new philosophic insights into the hidden possibilities of human personality enable us to look at life as a moving staircase leading us up from story to story in some super-department store. Shall we win the war? Of course. Shall we win the peace? Naturally. Will democracy survive? Who dares to doubt it? Is there a glorious future ahead for the human race? Surely! That is to say, all these bright prospects will be realized if we but take hold of ourselves, if only we become true persons and help others to become true persons. The possibilities are unlimited, if only we do not stand in our own way. And there is no reason why we should. Spengler was wrong. History does not move in hopeless cycles; history is linear; there are halts and detours, but still it goes onward and upward toward — toward something higher, we do not yet know what.

Of course Spengler was not altogether to blame for being so pessimistic in his day. The science of his time was pessimistic. It presented the view of hopeless mechanism. Not only nature but also the human body, and even the soul, were subject to pre-fixed, eternally immovable laws. Even religion in those days was pessimistic. It was authoritarian and exclusive. It dealt with creeds that required abject subjection of the human mind.

Even now there are mechanists in science and authoritarians in religion. Yet the dawn of a new day is breaking. Let us get up early to see the rising of the sun of joy for all, the sun of free personality.

I said there are mechanists in science and authoritarians in religion. But the authoritarians in religion are really the worst of mechanists. In fact the mechanism of the mechanists in science is not nearly so retarding to the rise of free personality as the mechanism of religion. It was the creation and providence doctrines of the old-fashioned religionists that were and are the only mechanism by which all things whatsoever come to pass according to a predetermined pattern. Well, we are virtually rid of that sort of thing now. I need not even argue against that. The great philosopher Immanuel Kant has shown, once for all, that all absolutes, such as the God of the orthodox theologians and the plan of this God, are merely to be taken as useful fictions to help us row our boats on the ocean of chance. "Just as in mathematics, the mathematical infinite presents a working principle exceedingly useful in achieving results, so there is an inner demand that morally and spiritually one must aim at perfection. The perfection aimed at can have no flaw, it must appear superhuman. These superhuman perfections are demanded as the attributes of God, the supreme reality" (p. 177). So we learn to use all the "omni" words, like omniscience and omnipresence, as merely negative indications of the field of pure possibilities where the reach of our understanding is exhausted. We are now no longer hemmed in by an all-encompassing God, but have the freedom of the seven seas. We now realize the "tentative and pragmatic nature of absolutes" in every direction (p. 178).

It only remains to warn the slower members of our fraternity not to long for the flesh-pots of Egypt. Mechanism in science is but a lingering scab of the boil of theological determinism that Kant has so effectively lanced. Some men, even some scientists, continue to think of causal law and the uniformity of nature as independent of the human mind. They have not realized the full import of Heisenberg's Principle of Indeterminacy and above all the significance of Planck's quantum theory (p. 201). Planck has worked out to its final consequence the principle of full control, on the part of the human person, over all significant possibility. "Planck has clearly shown that in nature we have not a continuous but an intermittent energy. These discontinuous impulses he calls *quanta*. If this is true it could be that *quanta* 'are issued as needed.' Their activity may spring out of or in accordance with a rational requirement. They may issue in response to a demand made by the general system of relations which calls them into being" (p. 202). Of course, to be polite we do not speak of our own individual minds as making nature and its laws. We rather absolutize our own minds in a figure and speak of a Supreme Mind as being the nexus of thought and thing. Yet we have accomplished a complete revolution in the interpretation of life. As the orthodox religionists interpret all things in terms of a self-existent and self-sufficient God and His plan, so we interpret all things in terms of a self-existent and self-sufficient man. Here lies our only hope of truly winning the war, the peace, democracy and a general future Utopia. "The human subject of experience is thus raised to a new dignity, since he is capable of gathering the discrete events into a meaningful whole" (p. 204). "Any philosophy or science which attempts to diminish or ignore the fact of man, however far it may throw a line into the universe, is guilty of the simplicity of one whale-fishing Simon, whose only ocean was in his mother's pail" (p. 280).

This gospel of free self-contained personality, Flewelling feels, is sure to be inherently acceptable to all the sons of men. There is a "higher self-forgetfulness" that marks all true men everywhere (p. 247). And religion must take the lead in opening the new door of progress to the human race. But once more is warning given that no institution of religion, no creed, no rite must be taken as the definition of religion here. "It is rather a living experience of God, a love for humanity, a devotion to righteousness so sincere that it will pay any price to bring in the true world order and in doing so will find its proper worship" (p. 248).

And if this should seem to lead us into a morass of contentless mysticism, into a vague sort of love of something somewhere, we may rest assured that where this sort of religion leads philosophy is sure to follow. In fact, such a religion of the free man worshipping himself must appeal to reason. "If religion is properly to meet the sweeping tides of change it is not enough that it should present only a mystical side. It must also appeal to the intellect. To this end it must call in again the service of philosophy as it has in the great periods of its past" (p. 251). A properly conditioned philosophy, that is, a philosophy worked out by the free personality, will tell us that all religions the wide world over have common *desiderata*.

Goodness, love, compassion, charity, uprightness, and so forth, are evidence to all men everywhere of the presence of the divine. And "if these are taken as the marks of God's presence in man it is possible to arrive at religious understanding and cooperation despite theological differences, for here we deal with the actual evidences of religion. Once these principles are recognized all else follows. Divinity is evidenced by indubitable testimony, the existence of perfect moral character, the life of perfect love in any religion" (p. 252). In this way philosophy can easily come to an "equitable appraisal of contrasting and even of contradictory ideas" (*ibid.*). No one takes his absolute so seriously as to think that he should actually be perfect in love. The only requirement for any man is that "he should honestly strive after it" (p. 178), and such striving is found everywhere. Between the Oriental who seeks for Nirvana and the personalist of California who seeks for self-denial there is seen to be no basic difference (p. 254). All will seek for the "supreme emotion" of self-sacrifice and speak the "universally understood language" of love (pp. 261 f.). Thus we have found the "neglected factor of progress" the factor which Spengler overlooked and of which orthodox Christianity has never caught the vision.

The present crisis of civilization, therefore, calls for true leadership, that is, true visual-mindedness. The world must become personalistic in the sense described, and with it cosmopolitan, or perish. We therefore appeal from the superficial laws of nature which Spengler dreaded so much as to pull out his hair in despair, and the far more dreadful theological plan of the orthodox God, to a deeper law of nature, to the law of human personality. "Let no one call this an appeal to magic, where natural forces have failed, for itself is a natural force", a natural force of larger sweep than we had dreamed (p. 238). We no longer look even in biology with hopeless conscript eyes for the "missing link". If the missing link be forever missing, we shall not miss it; we believe in evolution still. For evolution, the quantum theory now teaches, goes by jumps (p. 288). Why then not apply the same quantum theory boldly to history as a whole? Should a temporary downward trend to chaos make us fear lest we be engulfed forever? No, our little boat will weather the stormiest gale. Its bow may be washed with spray; it may dive into a wave and seem to disappear; the benighted provincialists of an antiquated religion may be ready to jump overboard and Spengler may bewail "the destiny of the West", but those who with the captain calmly dash into the wave will certainly emerge to a new and better day. "In the mental and spiritual organism of human society lies the possibility of never-ending and unlimited progress" (p. 297).

This is, in general terms, the optimistic picture Flewelling offers us as the substitute for that of Spengler's *The Decline of the West*. But such optimism is even more pessimistic than the pessimism of Spengler. It cannot even be presented with respectable logical consistency by such an able and accomplished philosopher as Dr. Flewelling undoubtedly is. All systems and creeds are to be set aside and personality to be put into their place. The idea of personality is to replace that of final systems. This point is made repeatedly. But then when personality is to tell us what it means by itself, it has to do so by appealing to the "common tests of reason" (p. 253). And therewith system returns. It is the *system* of personalist philosophy with which we deal. Flewelling speaks of the complementary character of systems. The idea of paradox is to help the lovers of system to sit peacefully planning together for a better world ruled only by love. But, in the end, the personalist system, now christened the "Christian system", is absolutely exclusive of historic Christianity. Thus a personalistic philosophy, averse to systems or tolerant and inclusive of all systems as complementary of one another, is utterly exclusive of the one system that is really a system and that is really a Christian system, namely, orthodox theology or, more specifically, the Reformed Faith.

Still further, finding so slim an intellectual foundation for his philosophy of optimism, Flewelling jumps from the intellect to the will and from the will to the emotion in human personality as his final courts of appeal. He tells us that religion alone has the will to make possible the new world order based on love; it alone will call forth the sacrifice required (p. 248). Here the will to believe, whatever the intellect may say, is made the basis of all. Secondly, he tells us that an impartial philosophy must provide the basis for a common understanding and a common striving for love (p. 249). Here the intellect, ignoring will and feeling alike, is made the final court of appeal. Finally, we are told that "in the emotional plane alone can men of varying interests, intelligences, habits, colors, creeds, occupations, come together and act together" (p. 259). We need therefore to find the "supreme emotion" more basic than either will or intellect. Thus, while reason, will and emotion are by turn made the final court of appeal, they are also said to be supplemental to one another. Flewelling is unable to come to any consistent point of view on the nature of human personality, which is made the basis for all his optimism. The weakness of his philosophy of optimism cannot be designated as due to either excessive emotionalism or excessive voluntarism, as over against a proper emphasis on the priority of the intellect. Flewelling is no more irrationalist than he is rationalist. To be sure, he is irrationalist, but he is also rationalist. Flewelling is emotionalist, voluntarist and intellectualist by turn, and he is all three at the same time.

A personalist philosophy such as Flewelling champions could not well result in anything else. Its chief trouble is that it has no intelligible meaning for the word "personality". Or, if we wish, we may say that the chief and final failure of personalism is its impersonalism. Not that personalism is more impersonalist than the avowed impersonalisms against which Flewelling makes war. His position is not worse and may even, in a sense, be said to be better than that of many of his opponents. But our contention is that only the historic Christian position, the position that, according to Flewelling, is the most impersonal of impersonalisms, is the true personalist philosophy. It is only in historic Christianity that the highest interpretative principle of philosophy is identified with the absolute personality of God.

Basic to the whole of the historic Christian position is the notion of the self-contained, triune, personal God. All of man's dealings, all of his thoughts, all of his emotions and all of his acts of will, in the final analysis, terminate upon the plan of this God. When human personality is normal it thinks God's thoughts after Him, wills God's will after Him, and loves God's love after Him, and all on a created plane. Human personality may, accordingly, be said to be, by nature, covenant personality. When this personality acts in accordance with the "system" of God it has true freedom for the exercise of all its functions; it is then fruitful to the glory of God in all that it does. It then deals with reality; it is assured of progress and the fulfillment of its talents.

When, however, this personality becomes abnormal through disobedience it seeks for the sort of freedom that Flewelling depicts so eloquently and so hopelessly. Refusing to live and move in the reality of God's counsel and its historical product in history, it seeks for a false frame of reference in itself as ultimate. Hence all the tears. Hence the narrow intellectualisms, voluntarisms and emotionalisms. Flewelling has dealt with human personality as a child might with a flower, first tearing off the leaves and then tying them on with a string, turning to its mother with great glee and optimistically predicting the wonderful results his plant is sure to produce. Flewelling has assumed that the abnormal sinful personality is normal, and in this assumption there is hidden a still deeper one to the effect that the finite person is not really finite but ultimate. In short, he has cut man loose from God and thus not only neglected, but self-consciously set aside, the one factor for progress on which rests the hope for the human race in our day.

Spengler's book met with vigorous protest from the Christian press.

Flewelling's book is not likely to do so. Even orthodox Christians are easily taken in by the high-sounding, apparently Christian terminology that such a personalism throws about like confetti on the religious multitude. Yet there can be no doubt that the personalism of Flewelling, like that of such men as Brightman and Knudson to which such frequent appeal is made for some support on the part of believing Christians, is just as destructive of Christianity as any materialism or mechanism ever was or is. When men forsake the historic Christian religion they invariably bound back and forth between a pessimism like that of Spengler and an optimism like that of Flewelling. From the Christian point of view both systems bring men and civilizations down to the Stygian darkness of scepticism and to the chains of the dwellers of Plato's cave. Here is that one Simon whale-fishing again in his mother's pail, only his mother's pail is now his mother's tea-cup.

There is, in all this, one obvious challenge. It is that of the training of the children of Christian parents in the understanding and practice of true covenant personality. If as Christians we are to meet the utter pessimism of the "optimism" of Flewelling, if we are as Christians to do our bit toward saving and founding democracy on a true basis, we shall need to train our children so that their personality develops harmoniously toward the self-conscious acceptance of their covenant relationship with their Creator and Redeemer.

Wilbur M. Smith: *Therefore, Stand.* Boston: W. A. Wilde Co. 1945. xxiv, 614. $3.00.

The volume before us seeks to offer "a plea for a vigorous apologetic in this critical hour of the Christian Faith". It aims to defend in particular the Biblical doctrines of creation, of the resurrection of Christ and of His final return to judgment. In doing so the author would follow the example of the apostle Paul in his Athenian address.

The argument on these three great doctrines is placed in a broad context. We are first made acquainted with the nature of the weapons with which the enemy attacks Christianity in our day (p. xiv). We are shown what great inroads the foes of Christianity have made on Christian territory and how the forces of evangelicalism seem to have been well-nigh driven into the sea. Unbelief is rampant in the modern world (pp. 1–202).

There are, of course, causes for this general unbelief. The natural man has a "bias against God" (p. 143). His mind is in darkness (pp. 147 ff.). Men have determined to live without God (p. 153). They have conditioned their children to do the same (p. 156). They have set too great store by material things; science has become their god (p. 160). Living in sin they refuse to believe (pp. 165 ff.). And back of all, there is the ever present influence of Satan and his servants (p. 175). As a result they have fallen into pessimism and despair (pp. 187–202).

The main argument of the book now begins to take shape. Still preparatory to it is a chapter dealing with Greek civilization "that we might realize anew the similarity between the age of the glory of Athens and our own intellectual age" (p. xv). It was to the Greeks that Paul came with his teachings on the doctrines of creation, resurrection and final judgment. Will Athens, compelled as she is by the sense of her own inadequacy to worship the unknown god, accept the God who has made the heavens and the earth? (p. 263). "Athens knew about everything that was knowable, except the most important things: she did not know God, she did not know what to do with her sins . . ." (p. 265). Will she accept the resurrection of Christ and His return to judgment if by revelation she is told of them? And in accepting them will she repent? And if we present the doctrines of creation, resurrection and judgment to the men of our age, will they accept them and repent?

At any rate we must make the same high claim that was made by Paul. We must tell men that they will remain suspended in chaos and contradiction if they do not accept the fact of creation (p. 289), and that they might as well believe the earth to be flat as deny the fact of Christ's resurrection (p. 406). We must also tell them that "no one can raise a reasonable objection, say from the laws of logic or the demands of the human heart against a final and universal judgment of God upon men who persist in breaking His laws" (p. 457).

Let us note how the author makes good these high claims he makes. His argument for creation may be summed up in the following quotation: "If there is such a thing as cause and effect and, thus, there is such a thing as cause, as all will agree, and if it seems reasonable from causes for all things that we seek to ascend to a First Cause, as the originator of this universe, then the creation account in Genesis is not only reasonable, and acceptable, but it sets forth a truth to which logic inevitably leads us" (p. 284).

There are, to be sure, those who are determined to say that there is no cause. Such will have to find some other theory "illogical as it may be, to account for the universe in which we live" (*idem*). There may also be those who even deny the existence of the universe but "with the intricate, fantastic, irrational theories concerning the *non-reality* of this great universe, and of life itself, we have no time in a world like this . . ." (pp. 272 f.). As realists we discuss only such things as "all our senses, and the very laws of logic, compel us to believe . . ." (p. 273). Beginning thus we soon discover with G. D. Hicks that "we cannot be condemned forever to the mere treadmill exercise of an indefinite regress" and come ultimately upon a reality "that is there, so to speak, in its own right" (p. 291). Nor need we fear to present the idea of creation as reasonable because we cannot show it to be wholly explicable. With F. R. Tennant we may say: " 'Some ultimates, analysable [should read "*un*analysable"] and unassimilable, there must be. Theism needs but to allow that creation is one of them' " (p. 282). Scientists themselves ought to be quite ready to accept the creation doctrine. Do they not unanimously confess that science "can tell us *nothing* about the *origin* of the world in which we live . . ."? (p. 273). "In other words, what science cannot discover, scientists long to know" (p. 275).

There follows an extensive discussion of the Genesis record, a comparison of the Biblical account of creation with non-Biblical accounts, a criticism of the idea of logical derivation. We cannot speak of these matters further. The value and validity of all of this material depends in large measure upon the validity of the main point in the argument for creation. It is this main argument that we have brought to the fore.

Essential to the author's defence of the resurrection of Christ is his distinction between fact and meaning. "The *meaning* of the resurrection

is a theological matter, but the fact of the resurrection is a historical matter
. . ." (p. 386). In his argument, therefore, he deals primarily with the
fact of the resurrection. To convince men of the fact he deals at length
with the empty tomb and the post-resurrection appearances. Living in a
day when "the value of historical certainty is dogmatically insisted upon"
(p. 359), we can give men an abundance of the sort of evidence they seek
when investigating any other subject (p. 389). Since, then, the proof for
the resurrection of Christ is so abundant and so wholly in accord with
the modern scientific demand for proof we may call upon young men to
take a stand upon it and accept it in its full significance (p. 430). "To
reject the Resurrection is to go against every law of logic which man has
discovered." Not only that, it is virtually to reject the whole of Christian
teaching (p. 437). It is to "put out the one great light that can illuminate
our future" (*idem*).

The question of the final judgment is treated far more compendiously
than either that of creation or the resurrection of Christ. Is there evidence
for a final judgment as compelling as that for creation and the resurrection
of Christ? In the chapter on creation the author found the fact of creation
which *everybody*, barring a few extremists, accepted, to be a well-graded
runway from which he could take off with men and reach God as the Creator of the world. In the chapter on the resurrection he found a similar
point of contact in the fact that the evidence for the resurrection is exactly
the same sort of evidence as scientists demand when seeking knowledge
in any field. In the first case, theists and non-theists have the concept
of causality in common. In the second case, they have the concept of
evidence in common. It is on this identity of content of the concepts of
causation and evidence as between theists and non-theists, or Christians
and non-Christians, that the author rests his case when seeking to make
good his high claim for creation and the resurrection of Christ. Is there
a similar point of contact in the minds of men in general for the idea of a
final judgment?

It is a little difficult to determine the author's meaning at this point.
We are told that "apart from the Word of God we know absolutely nothing
about a future judgment" (p. 446). This would seem to preclude the hope
of a point of contact with those who do not accept the Scriptures as the
Word of God. However, the author does seem to find a point of contact
after all in the general idea of judgment. "Whatever one may think of
the truth or falsehood of a final, universal, righteous judgment by God,
no one can possibly deny the fact that judgment itself is an inescapable,
daily experience, individually and corporately, for all mankind" (pp. 439

f.). There is also the testimony of men's hearts to a judgment to come (p. 451). "Judgment is not only a scriptural doctrine. It is the inevitable, inescapable end of history, if there is anywhere ruling in this world a righteous God" (p. 455). The "laws of logic", then, and "the demands of the human heart" seem not merely to agree with what Scripture teaches about a final judgment day, but seem of themselves to demand what is there taught. Moreover, the orthodox apologists may be encouraged by such theologians as Barth and Reinhold Niebuhr who have "brought into sharp focus . . . this inevitableness of final judgment" (p. 460). As we realize, then, that we need to preach this doctrine of the judgment with the authority of the Word of God we are comforted with the fact that "this need is exactly what is recognized among some of the outstanding leaders of thought of our day" (p. 462) who do not base their thinking upon the infallible Word at all. Having found a common meeting place with those whom we seek to win to a belief in a final judgment in the identity of concept that we have, both as to judgments in history and as to the human heart and its basic moral demands, we can press our claims with confident hope of acceptance. Thus, then, on the question of a final judgment as well as on those of creation and of the resurrection of Christ we may still carry on a vigorous apologetic. We need only to push men to accept the logical conclusions of concepts they have themselves embraced. Having accepted the fact and concept of cause, they ought logically to accept the fact of a Creator. Having accepted a concept of evidence by which they satisfy themselves of the actual existence of the realities of the world, they ought logically also to accept the resurrection of Christ. Finally, having accepted the fact of judgment as seen in history and as required by the moral consciousness of man, they ought logically to accept a final judgment of all men by Christ.

For an understanding of the author's argument it is important to note that he is not appealing to something in men that is hidden underneath their professed positions. He is appealing to the conceptions of cause, of evidence and of judgment that men have self-consciously formed for themselves. The distinction between what men say they believe in their professed positions and what, deep in their hearts, they believe in spite of their own professions is not introduced anywhere in the book. The argument may accordingly be said to be basically similar to that of Bishop Butler in his *Analogy*. Both Butler and Smith would simply ask men to be consistent with themselves and to apply the principles of interpretation that they have already successfully employed in one field to a field that is new to them. The chief difference, apart from details, between the procedure of Butler and that of Smith seems to be that Smith makes higher claims than Butler did. Butler felt that men had done justice to the evidence if they concluded that God did probably exist and Christianity was probably true, whereas Smith boldly affirms that men ought to conclude that Christian theism is certainly true.

Our evaluation of the book under discussion may accordingly begin by affirming our agreement with the author when, in distinction from Butler, he asserts that of the creation of the world, of the resurrection of Christ and of His final judgment men ought to have no doubt. The evidence for these doctrines, as for the whole Christian scheme of things, is abundantly clear. In expounding Scripture, and especially St. Paul, Calvin has made this point quite clear. No apologetic argument dare omit or ignore this basic fact. It is equally clear, however, that the natural man refuses to see any fact in the universe, and therefore the universe as a whole, for what it really is. Calvin, again following Paul, is as insistent on this point as on the former. Men's professed positions are the means by which they "keep under" or cover up the truth about themselves and the facts about them. This is true even when in these professed positions they say what is formally true. Deep down in their hearts men have the sense of deity; deep down they know they are God's creatures and that God is the creator of the universe in its totality. Yet in their professed positions they assume the non-createdness of themselves and of the world at large. Deep down in their hearts they know that they are sinners before the Creator God and that judgment awaits them. Yet in their professed position they reduce good and evil to correlatives of one another.

In refusing to make the distinction between what men profess to believe and what they believe deep in their hearts the author has chosen to follow Butler rather than Calvin and Paul. This is a matter of great disappointment. Butler failed to prove by his method that Christianity is probably true; how much the more must one fail if one seeks by a similar method to show that it is certainly true. This is not to say that much of the material employed by the author is not good and apologetically valuable. But it is to say that there is in the book no adequate organizational principle by means of which the material can be made to tell its story in a truly effective way.

The only organizing principle commensurate with the needs of the occasion is to be found in the position defended. If Christianity is to be defended as certainly, rather than probably, true, as the only reasonable religion rather than as a mere faith-construct, this must be done, we believe, by showing that nothing, either in logic or in fact, is intelligible to man except in terms of Christianity's basic principles and differentiations. If logic, to be fruitfully employed, can be shown to require as its presupposition the Creator-creature distinction as this is maintained in the orthodox faith, then, and then only, dare we say to men that it is illogical not to accept the Christian position. If the concept of fact can be shown to be unintelligible except upon the presupposition of the counsel of God as controlling whatsoever comes to pass, then, and then only, dare we say to men that it is out of accord with fact not to accept the Christian position.

Smith assumes that Christians and non-Christians mean the same thing when they speak of causation within the universe. He urges those who accept the fact of causation within the universe to be consistent with themselves and therefore to accept, also, the fact of the causation of the whole universe. That is the burden of his argument. But Aristotle did accept the fact of causation and he also accepted the idea of a first cause. And the author himself points out that the first cause of which Aristotle speaks is not the God of Christianity. Was then the father of logic illogical? We do not think so. He was strictly consistent with himself. The kind of first cause he believed in accords exactly with the kind of causation concept he spoke of as operative within the universe.

Or again, it is of the essence of post-Kantian phenomenalism to assume that time and chance are ultimate. This notion of the ultimacy of chance is one of the ingredients of its concept of causation. Such is the case with the work of G. Dawes Hicks to which Smith refers. Hicks argues that those who believe in causation within the universe should logically also believe in a first cause. While asserting his belief in a first cause, however, he specifically affirms that it must not be causation "in the strict sense of that phrase. For if it were, it would imply either a change in something already existing other than God, or else a change in God Himself, whereby from a condition of non-creativeness God passed into one of creativeness. And each of these alternatives is clearly contradictory."[1] And on his assumptions Hicks is right. To ask men merely to be consistent with themselves when they have accepted the fact of causation within the universe usually means not to ask them to see the Christian position as certainly true, nor even to ask them to see it as probably true; it is to ask them to see that it is not true at all.

In the chapter on the resurrection of Christ Smith again seeks for com-

[1] *The Philosophical Bases of Theism*, New York, 1937, p. 176.

mon or neutral ground. This time he finds it in the common notion of historical evidence. If, then, men will only apply their accepted method of historical investigation they ought to accept the fact of Christ's resurrection. Could not the risen body of our Lord be touched with human hands and seen with human eyes? (p. 389). But Smith does not make clear how, if scientists would accept the fact of the risen Jesus on the basis of their own principles of evidence, they should also logically accept this Jesus as the Christ, the Son of God. Nor could he do so. On the commonly accepted concept of historical evidence in post-Kantian science, no fact can be accepted as a fact with scientific standing unless it is an essentially repeatable instance of a law that finds its ultimate reference point in man. Having misinterpreted every other historical fact by such a method, why should men suddenly make an exception and look at the resurrection of Christ for what it really is? When, therefore, we ask men to be consistent with their own principles of historical evidence and merely to apply these principles to the fact of Christ's resurrection, we are really asking them to remain true to their initial error in order that they may thus escape ever being confronted with the real resurrection of Christ.

As already suggested, the argument on the final judgment is not as clear as that on the two subjects discussed. Yet here, also, the author seems to base his apologetic argument on a general concept of judgment concerning which the general moral consciousness of man agrees. The courts in every civilized country recognize the necessity of punishment for personal crimes. The last war has convinced men that international crimes must also be punished. How then can they logically raise any objection to a final punishment? (p. 457). If men believe in the fact of punishment within the universe, why should they not believe in a final punishment for wicked men at the end of all history? But, we ask, why do men believe in the fact of judgment? More often than not, it is because they think it useful for the evolutionary progress of the race. It is not because they think that, as God's image-bearers, men have broken the laws of their Creator. For such men the whole course of history runs without God. Why then should they think of God as having anything to do with the end of history? In fact, why should they think of an end of history at all? The author speaks of Karl Barth as teaching the "inevitableness of judgment" (p. 460). But Barth asserts emphatically that eschatology has nothing to do with dates on a calendar. For Barth, the creation of the world, the resurrection of Christ, and his return to final judgment are alike non-historical. To be sure, as a merely limiting concept or faith-construct, men such as Barth and Reinhold Niebuhr may logically believe in a final judgment, but their basic principles of theology do not permit of a judgment at the end of time. It follows, then, that to ask men who believe in the fact of judgment within history simply to be consistent with themselves and also to believe in a final judgment at the end of history, is usually to ask them, in effect, to make an illogical jump or else to reject altogether the final judgment as orthodox theology thinks of it.

Much then as we may approve of the high aims of the book before us, and much as we may admire the industry that has gone into its making, we are bound to indicate that a general evangelical apologetic, inasmuch as it is bound to concede the autonomy of man to some extent, is not adequate for our day. A really "vigorous apologetic" must spring directly from a vigorous theology and must in its method be the direct implicate of such a theology. When setting forth their system of theology, Reformed theologians are anxious to be true to Scripture and, therefore, to make no concessions to the demands of the natural man. They are vigorously critical of Arminianism, though highly appreciative of good men who are Arminians, because they are convinced that it makes concessions to the natural man, and thus is virtually the hole in the dike through which the waters of naturalism may come to inundate the gospel of God's free grace as proclaimed in the church of Christ. Why then should not Reformed theologians at least strive to develop a method of apologetic argument that dares to face the natural man and challenge the correctness of his interpretations of facts within the universe no less than of facts pertaining to the universe as a whole? In theology, men insist that all facts and all concepts of men have their meaning and are intelligible because of their ultimate reference point in the self-contained sovereign God. How dare they allow, in apologetics, that men are right in their conception of facts even when they make the would-be autonomous man the ultimate reference point of predication?

One thing, at least, seems to be clear. A generally evangelical apologetic to a large extent defeats its own purposes. True enough much good may be accomplished, both by an Arminian theology and by a generally evangelical method of apologetic. In this fact all who love the Lord will rejoice. But how much more good may be accomplished by the grace of God through a more consistently Biblical theology and a more consistently Biblical apologetic. A generally evangelical apologetic does not drive the natural man into a corner with no hope of escape. It does not track him down till he is at bay. It does not destroy his last shelter. His fire is not altogether extinguished. There always remains to him, even by permission of the soldiers of the cross, the right to undermine the work of God. If then the heart of man is desperately wicked, it will not fail to use the instrument of consistency and claim the right to reject the central facts of Christian theism. A plea for a vigorous apologetic ought therefore to be a plea for a genuinely Reformed apologetic. We may not be clear, indeed, as to the full implications of a truly Reformed apologetic. But this fact does not justify us in refusing to point out to those who, with us, love the Christian Faith that a generally evangelical apologetic, like a Roman Catholic apologetic, is inadequate for any time and especially inadequate for our time.

G. C. Berkouwer: *Dogmatische Studiën. Geloof en Rechtvaardiging.* Kampen: J. H. Kok. 1949. 220. f. 4.95.

G. C. Berkouwer: *Dogmatische Studiën. Geloof en Heiliging.* Kampen: J. H. Kok. 1949. 222. f. 4.95.

The author of these volumes is already well and favorably known among those who are interested in the spread of the full-orbed gospel of saving grace. He has written several important works in evaluation and criticism of Romanism and of Crisis Theology. Even from his doctoral dissertation (*Geloof en Openbaring in de Nieuwere Duitsche Theologie*) it was apparent that he had made himself thoroughly familiar with the various schools of modern thought without being swept off his feet by any of them.

We are happy, therefore, that Dr. Berkouwer has projected a series of studies of a doctrinal nature. In nineteen volumes he plans to cover such subjects as the Dogma of the church, the Revelation of God, the Bible as the Word of God, Creation, Providence, Sin, the Comfort of Election, the Covenant of God, Christology, The Holy Spirit, Faith and Justification, the Church, Baptism, the Lord's Supper, the Kingdom of God and Eschatology.

In the first of the present volumes, which deals with faith and justification, the "sola fide"-"sola gratia" principle of the Reformation is stated afresh and set off clearly against ancient and especially against modern deviations and perversions of it.

Everything depends, Berkouwer argues, upon viewing faith and justification as genuinely correlative to one another. With constant and comprehensive reference to Scripture he indicates the nature of this correlativity. The sovereign grace of God is at the bottom of it (p. 168). Those who do not make the electing grace of God basic to the correlation between faith and justification are bound to ascribe merit to faith. On the other hand those who substitute the dialectical for the historically Reformed conception of election are bound to deny the significance of faith as an act of man for to them faith is really belief by God in God (p. 181). The real priority of the grace of God and the genuine historical significance of man's response in faith therefore rest upon the sovereign election of God.

There are many variations on this central theme of the book. The author shows that the ent're Bible, not only the letters of Paul, teaches both the absolute priority of grace and, at the same time, the absolute necessity of faith. He shows that the truly ethical concept of justification must be of a forensic or juridical nature. Denying the truly forensic nature of justification, Romanism has been unable to maintain the full Biblical doctrine of salvation by grace alone. Berkouwer indicates that James as well as Paul teaches justification by faith alone, that a judgment upon men's works is still a judgment on their faith. He shows that faith is "empty", is but an "instrument" but not a "crater" in the dialectical sense of the term. He shows that the orthodox rather than the dialectical view of justification is truly existential in character. The orthodox view does not pretend that man is able to penetrate the relation between God and man by his intellect; it is not *speculative* in character. On the other hand the orthodox view does not make a false contrast between Christianity as a set of intellectual propositions and Christianity as communication of reality; it is not irrational in character.

Other matters might be mentioned but these may suffice to indicate the truly Biblical and up-to-date character of the work before us. The author frankly builds upon the work of such great Reformed theologians as Kuyper and Bavinck but is not a slavish follower of their thought. In him Reformed theology has found an exponent worthy of its glory.

In the second of the volumes under consideration Dr. Berkouwer deals with the relation of faith to the process of sanctification. The Biblical doctrine of sanctification is clearly set forth. The Romanist and dialectical heresies are contrasted with Scriptural teaching. He who constantly keeps in mind the correlativity of faith and sanctification, Berkouwer argues, will not be either a perfectionist or an antinomian.

There is a particularly fine analysis of the "imitatio Christi" literature.

"There is an absolute priority of His grace" in our following of Christ's example (p. 152). Christ did not merely illustrate a general law of humility, but true human humility is founded on redemption through His mediatorial work (p. 155).

Berkouwer fears every form of reaction theology. The Romanist doctrine of infused grace led by way of reaction to antinomianism. He points out that true faith is bound to express itself in observance of the law of God. Sometimes he speaks of dialecticism as though it were merely a matter of reaction. It may be doubted whether such a movement as dialectical theology is adequately signalized in terms of reactionism. Berkouwer's own writings have done much to show that Karl Barth's theology is based upon a nominalist foundation. On such a basis no Christian theology is possible. There is merely a similarity of words between the doctrine of free grace as taught by Barth and as taught by the Reformed Faith. Barth's doctrine of the process of sanctification is therefore more than a false emphasis of the truth; it is a rejection of the truth.

ed. Edward D. Myers: *Christianity and Reason. Seven Essays.* New York: Oxford University Press. 1951. xv, 172. $3.00.

The Voice of the Center comes to expression once again in this volume. Dr. Theodore M. Greene of Yale speaks of his view as "liberal Christian Protestantism" (p. 14). This is, he thinks, Christianity "at its enlightened best" (p. 13). It is "committed to reliance upon scientific evidence and to the full incorporation of accepted scientifically supported interpretations of nature" (p. 9). But it is not narrow. It does not limit man's interest to the data of science only. Man's experience is not limited to sensory data. "What is to prevent us from being really empirical and believing that man's moral and religious experiences, which are no less coercive, vivid, sharable, and rationally interpretable than are his sensory experiences, provide further contacts with reality and further clues to its nature?" (p. 11). Thus the readers of Professor Walter Stace's article "Man Against Darkness" (*Atlantic Monthly*, September, 1948) may find themselves reassured for "man finds himself today not in 'darkness' but in a cultural and spiritual twilight which T. S. Eliot describes as a 'place of disaffection ... in a dim light,' a state of 'neither plenitude nor vacancy,' 'a twittering world' " (p. 16). More light than that the reader should be warned not to expect. For those who believe in the absolute authority either of a book or a church are claiming too much. Hold to a balanced view between extreme naturalism and extreme supernaturalism and you will walk in twilight.

If the reader has some misgivings about walking in the twilight he may turn to John Wild of Harvard. For Wild assures him that he does not regard "intellectual vagueness and compromise as a virtue" (p. 23). "On the other hand, it is clear insight into fixed first principles which alone enables us to meet the ever-changing contingencies of the concrete situation with a firm and guided flexibility" (*idem*). These fixed first principles he gets from the Greeks (*idem*). "Realism, rationalism, and the law of nature are three distinct but inseparable components of the central core of Western philosophy, I should say of any sound philosophy" (p. 28). They "can be seen to be true, and will stand up under the scrutiny of the individual intellect" (*idem*). And they are "in definite accord with dogmas of the faith" (*idem*). They are also the presupposition of the Christian faith (p. 31). Mankind starts with a "dim knowledge of the *Deus absconditus*". Natural theology, such as set forth in the principles just enumerated, clarifies and articulates this knowledge (*idem*). This gives man the clear insight into fixed first principles mentioned above. But this knowledge "tells us nothing of His (God's) inner, private life, so to speak, and of His personal attitude toward us" (*idem*). So there needs must be an "eruption of God Himself into the matter and flesh of human history" (*idem*). "The impact of this eruption was profound" (p. 32). Our human nature was "taken over by God himself in the Incarnation" (p. 28). Thus "an actual human life was lived and finished" (p. 32). And "through the sacraments, this life once lived was preserved and maintained within the Church, to be shared and corporately extended through oncoming generations" (pp. 32 f.).

"This great body of truth", Wild warns in conclusion, must be guarded "... against vagueness, eclectic confusion, and secular adulteration" (p. 35). Only then can it focus its light "upon the unprecedented problems of contemporary life" (*idem*).

Perhaps the reader will think that Wild has only added "vagueness, eclectic confusion, and secular adulteration" to the "twilight" offered him by Greene. If "the great eruption" of God results in the submerging of the divine life into human nature, does not this new human nature itself need a new eruption? A patient dying from leukemia may be given a blood transfusion. He may be given many blood transfusions. But he will die with the blood of these very "eruptions" in his body. A human nature not interpreted at the outset in terms of God the Creator cannot be redeemed by eruptions from the realm of the *Deus absconditus*.

But the reader must have patience. He must hear about the "mediating view" of George F. Thomas of Princeton University. Thomas would offer a natural theology more modest in its claims and more empirical than that of Thomas Aquinas (p. 42). Warmed with such an empirically founded natural theology he would then go direct to the "historical events" that gave rise to the doctrines of Christianity (p. 47). Thus reason must "take the responsibility of interpreting the meaning of the revelation independently in the light of the best Biblical scholarship and of religious experience and reflection" (p. 48). Thus the theologians may "speak from the center rather than the periphery of the Christian community" (p. 51). And thus he may expect to have "glimpses of truth now and then." and wait for the full vision of it in the life to come (p. 56).

If the reader should not be satisfied with these "glimpses of truth" offered him by Thomas and should seek to turn to the Bible as the infallible Word of God he may be warned by Wilbur Marshall Urban, again from Yale, that "the nemesis of extreme revelationalism is sure and certain" (p. 74). "In sum, any tenable doctrine of revelation presupposes an understanding of the relation of the Word of God to the word of man, and this in turn presupposes a relation of the human to the Divine which, in the last analysis, can be determined only by reason" (*idem*). Thus we are thrown back on reason again. It is to experience or reason, to empirical research by the accepted scientific method of investigation, that each writer takes us back. Lewis M. Hammond of the University of Virginia agrees with the writers already mentioned. And as Urban would hold to "symbolism as a theological principle" (p. 60), so Hammond would lead on "from univocal to . . . analogical signification of terms" (p. 91). The idea is that man by himself, without God, can correctly know the world about him and that he must think of what is beyond nature as being an analogy with that which he has already found in nature. And Howard Dykema Roelofs, of the University of Cincinnati, in reviewing the various papers of this book, concludes that the primary data of religious experience, and therefore of theological science, are inescapably ambiguous (p. 122). This is true, he thinks, because "what is revealed, although given to the subject, is yet received only by an interpretative response of the subject, and is in itself not an element in the order of nature" (p. 135). How then can man ever escape the fear that his knowledge of God is naught but an illusion? Cannot God break through this illusion and reach the heart of man with certainty that is clear and objective?

> Why has not God arranged it so that at least knowledge of His existence could be easily obtained, plainly and surely confirmed?
> Why not? While thinking on this, frequently with vexation and irritation, it finally did come to me that every difficulty we find in trying to obtain knowledge of God is a difficulty He encounters in making Himself plain to us. If He speaks it must be in our language, what we understand . . . . Every sign requires interpretation, and all interpretations are ambiguous (p. 143).

Thus we are back with Stace's "Man Against Darkness" again. Even the twilight and the glimmerings promised us have finally disappeared; no real answer is given and on the basis of operation adopted in this book no answer to Stace could be given. For man's reason, man's whole interpretative power is not first interpreted in terms of the God of Christianity. The primary data of religion, human reason and its criteria of operation, in short, the whole of the procedure of human knowledge is first taken as though it were intelligible without God and is then set to work on the task of finding God. It is, of course, quite consistent, then, to say that God has great trouble in making himself known to man. Thus it is God that is blamed for man's ignorance of him and the sinner has found a new excuse for his failure to serve him. Thus is the Voice of the Center leading back from Protestantism to Romanism and then to paganism.

REVIEWS OF BOOKS

Alan Richardson: *Christian Apologetics*. New York and London: Harper & Brothers. 1947 .56. $3.00.
Edward John Carnell: *An Introduction to Christian Apologetics*. Grand Rapids: W. B. Eerdmans Publishing Co. 1948. 379. $3.50.

The two books under review represent two opposite points of view both as to the nature and the defence of Christianity. We may therefore think of them as engaged in debate and watch for results.

Representing the modern point of view, Richardson naturally contends that "Christian apologetics must inevitably raise the question of the methodology of theological science in relation to that of the sciences in general". Theology must submit its claims "to the test of scientific method" (p. 7).

In masterly fashion the author acquits himself of his task. Revelation, he argues, is not a figment of the imagination of theologians but "a category based upon observable facts and recognizable experiences" (p. 21). And when the Christian intimates the nature of his approach to Reality by saying, *Credo ut intelligam*, he does what the adherent of the best philosophy also does. What is more, the "biblical faith-principle" appears to be the highest, the most unifying, hypothesis for the explanation of life that man can find.

Richardson insists that his position be distinguished from that of classical rationalism. His view, he says, allows him to accept the "scandal of particularity" and the mystery of election. Special revelation is "revelation in and through history". Then too his position allows him to say with Augustine that all human knowledge needs the illumination of God.

That Richardson's view of Christianity is typical of our time scarcely needs to be established. One need only to think of such names as Niebuhr, Kroner, Tillich, Ferré, Mackay and Homrighausen to realize this fact. But that for all its stress upon the "uniqueness" of Christianity and for all its "Augustinianism" this view implies the complete rejection of historic Christian theism seems not to be generally recognized. Not as though Richardson himself seeks in any wise to hide his hostility to the orthodox

Christian Faith. He informs us plainly that "there are no such things as 'absolute perspectives' in existential matters" (p. 107). The Christian perspective is the best perspective we know of now.

Not so long ago orthodox apologetics was wont to defend its position by the "you also" method. Does Christianity depend upon faith? so does science and so does philosophy. To use this method now would lead to nothing but confusion. Philosophers and scientist now vie with one another in their acceptance of the "unique" and the mysterious. There is, moreover, not merely a "return to religion" but a "return to Calvinism". For all that, the rejection of orthodox Christianity is as violent as ever.

It is imperative, then, that the two faith-principles themselves be compared with one another. The old and the new conceptions of "uniqueness", as well as the old and the new forms of Augustinianism, must be set over against one another.

But this very thing it is that the traditional method of orthodox apologetics, still so much in vogue, is unable to do. Traditional apologetics is committed to a methodology which is not Augustinian in either the historic or the modern sense of the term. It is thereby virtually bound to deny the significance of the contrast between the two types of Augustinianism. On the principles of Thomas Aquinas and Bishop Butler "reason" and "faith" mean virtually the same thing for the Christian and the non-Christian. How then could a Romanist, or a follower of Butler, meet a position such as that of Richardson?

The only recourse of the traditional apologist is an appeal to balance. Sensing the fact that Richardson's conception of uniqueness is obtained at the expense of all rationality he might use the argument so commonly employed since Hegel's day to the effect that uniqueness apart from system is without intelligible meaning. Following T. H. Green he might show how pure empiricism must lead to scepticism. On the other hand, sensing the fact that on Richardson's conception of universal coherence all historic uniqueness disappears, he might use the argument so commonly employed since Kierkegaard's day that coherence or system, without content derived from pure uniqueness, is also without intelligible meaning.

It is apparent, however, that in both cases Richardson would agree. It is difficult to conceive of a nicer balance than that found in his book. But then it is a balance between pure rationalism and pure irrationalism. Post-Kantian phenomenalism, whether in theology or in philosophy and science, consists precisely in the delicacy with which it seeks to satisfy both Parmenides and Heraclitus. And failing to challenge the common assumption of both, traditional orthodox apologetes were never able to challenge either rationalism or irrationalism effectively. The most they were able, at any time in the past, to accomplish was to hold out for a balance between them and call it "analogy of being".

But if orthodoxy has always been largely at the mercy of its foes because of its failure, and even unwillingness, to work out its own apologetic methodology, that fact ought now to be more apparent than ever. There is nothing that the traditional method of Aquinas or Butler could present that would really tell against the position of Richardson. That position is a well high perfect balance between the *a priori* and *a posteriori* forms of reasoning as these have frequently been employed by orthodox Christian apologists.

* * * *

As already suggested the only way in which Richardson's position may be really challenged is by showing that a non-Christian *a priori* cannot save from scepticism and that a non-Christian *a posteriori* cannot produce true historical individuality, while the balanced combination of these two but hides from the unwary the defects of both.

But then it is only on the presupposition of the truth of historic Calvinism that this can be accomplished. It is only if God by his counsel really controls whatsoever comes to pass that we have a true Augustinianism, a true *a priori*. For then the mind of man is required to think of its moulding of the facts of history into a "system" as at every point analogous to the prior and ultimate ordering of these facts by God. Then, too, we have the true idea of uniqueness, a uniqueness consisting in the precise place that anything in the universe occupies by virtue of the plan of God. Thus to presuppose the self-sufficiency of God, thus to maintain the actual control of all historic factuality by the plan of God is to exercise the historic Augustinian faith-principle in our times.

But such Augustinianism is identical with Calvinism. And this will at once indicate the necessity of dropping once for all the appeal to categories accepted by believers and unbelievers alike. It is precisely on the nature of the most fundamental categories of interpretation that the true historic and the modern pseudo-Augustinianism are most profoundly at variance with one another. To appeal to "logic", that is to the "law of contradiction", or to "experience" and "facts" as such, is worse than merely confusing. It is these categories themselves that are in dispute. To argue about a position as being "in accord with logic" and as being "in accord with fact" is to beat the air and thus to fail to present the challenge of the Christian position at all. Really to challenge men with the truth of

Christianity is to deal with logic and with facts, showing that the two have their relevance on Christian presuppositions alone.

Turning now to Carnell's book, the question is whether, in seeking to vindicate orthodox Christianity, Carnell has continued to follow traditional methodology with all its fatal weaknesses or has developed a more consistently Christian, and therefore a more effective, approach. The answer to this question is not easy to find. Sometimes he comes out boldly with the Christian challenge, contending that unless one presupposes the infallible Scripture, with the system of doctrine it contains, there is no rationality in any human experience. Then again, he relies on a vague sort of Platonic or even Cartesian *a priorism* to bring unity into human experience.

In evidence of the former such points as the following may be mentioned.

Without any hesitation he takes the highest possible position with respect to the question of authority: "Christianity assumes the existence of the God Who has revealed Himself in Scripture to solve both metaphysical and epistemological problems" (p. 96). Or again: "The Christian, having chosen as his logical starting point the existence of the God Who has revealed Himself in Scripture, is admonished, as an implication of this starting point, to hue (*sic*) to the implications of this decision in every phase of life" (p. 212).

It is the sovereign God who speaks in Scripture. "Being contingent upon God's will, it is this will, and not an antecedent system of logic, which gives meaning to the movement of the time-space world" (p. 40). It is therefore by an act of this sovereign God that men learn to accept Him and His revelation for what they are: "The power by which the heart is enabled to see that the word of God is true is the Holy Spirit. The word of God is thus self-authenticating. It bears its own testimony to truth; it seals its own validity" (p. 66). "The surest proof one can have that his faith in God's word is valid is the internal witness of the Spirit of God in his heart" (p. 68).

In all this we have historic Augustinianism. To have a "whole-soul trust in God's word as true" (p. 66) and to mean by this that one believes in the Bible as infallibly revealing an existential system is something abhorrent to the "Augustinianism" of Richardson. Believing in the total depravity of the mind of fallen man (p. 279) Carnell speaks of the "complete penetration into our inward lives that sin enjoys" (p. 199). Speaking of men in general he says: "But, being in defection by their sins, what they see is vitiated. Thus, they are not able to see and appreciate that one of the peculiar characteristics of this God is that He is the Creator of the world and the Savior of men" (p. 171).

How then, Carnell virtually asks, can there be a common basis of argument between believers and unbelievers? The "Christian operates under *one* major premise — the existence of the God Who has revealed Himself in Scripture" (p. 175). "The Christian denies the competency of man's mind to know reality without revelation, while the non-Christian confesses it" (p. 201). How shall the Christian, then, reason with one whose major premise is the self-sufficiency of the human mind? The Christian must be alert to the danger that the "enemy" likes to "fix" the game. "If the Christian is disqualified from the arena by rules which his opponent makes, it is evident that the game has been 'fixed' " (pp. 94 f.). An orthodox Christian ought therefore not to argue with his opponent on "common ground". For on this "common ground" the enemy has "fixed" the rules of the game. "If we try to come to the Bible with a principle of selectivity found outside of the Bible, we render the Bible needless, since we can accept of it only what coincides with the truth which we had before we ever came to Scripture in the first place" (p. 198).

What then should the Christian do? He should argue that unless one presupposes the truth of the existential system revealed in Scripture one drops into scepticism (p. 97). The Bible's message "stands pitted in judgment against" the scientific method of its critics (p. 194). "Technically speaking, whenever a man talks and expects something to be meant by it, he is resorting to a prerogative which belongs to the Christian alone. On an empirical flux system, one can only, like Cratylus, wave his hand to express his philosophy, for from flux and change only flux and change can come" (p. 212). It is thus that Carnell sets off the true Augustinian faith-principle from the false. With full confidence the true principle challenges the false. The challenge is made on the point of the principle of individuation. The false faith-principle of Richardson posits chance as the source of space-time factuality. Carnell's faith-principle posits God's promise as the reason for the regularity of the seasons (p. 53). The challenge is also made at the most crucial point — the place of the mind of man in one's life and world view. The false faith-principle of Richardson in effect denies the created and fallen character of the human mind. The faith-principle of Carnell says that "the creature-Creator relationship is inviolable" (p. 185). The former seeks its coherence by means of abstract principles of logic above gods and men; the latter seeks for coherence by reformulating the facts of God's revelation according to the principles of Scripture.

* * * *

But, the careful reader of Carnell's book will ask, are you really presenting Carnell's main approach in thus stressing the difference between the true and the false Augustinianism? That there is a legitimate doubt on this matter may be briefly indicated as follows.

We have seen how Scripture is said to be self-authenticating and its reception by the sinner as absolutely true as due to the internal witness of the Spirit. But this high position is not maintained. It is not made to count as basic in the argument. It is even openly rejected and flouted. Self-authenticating Scripture is asked to give "rational evidences of its authority" (p. 71). Reason, not as interpreted by Scripture but as taken by those not believing in Scripture, is authorized "to canvass the evidence of a given authority" (p. 72). "When one comes averring to be from God, it surely is a man's duty to demand a proof that this is so" (p. 268 f.). "Bring on your revelations! Let them make peace with the law of contradiction and the facts of history, and they will deserve a rational man's assent" (p. 178). And the Christian apologist is presented as being glad to take the test as set by an autonomous reason, "A careful examination of the Bible reveals that it passes these stringent examinations *summa cum laude*" (p. 178). "The Conservative" now forgets to make the creature-Creator relationship primary. He forgets his doctrine of total depravity. For fear that he shall be classed with the mystics and sceptics, he hastens to explain that, after all, his final appeal is not "to *ipse dixit* authority, but to coherent truth" (p. 72). After all, "the Reformation stemmed from a sanctified application of systematic consistency to the teachings of the Roman Catholic church" (p. 73). "Any theology which rejects Aristotle's fourth book of the Metaphysics is big with the elements of its own destruction" (pp. 77 f.). Though our logical starting point is the Trinity we realize that "all logical ultimates must be tested" and that "the only way to do this is to work out a still more primitive starting procedure" (p. 124). And here we gladly turn with you to Plato. Carnell's "Conservative" is glad to substitute a Platonic *a priori* for the *tabula rasa* empiricism of the Thomist. In his doctrine of the image of God, the "Conservative" has the justification for the identification of his own *a priori* with that of Plato. "But that Plato hit upon the right synoptic starting point can be explained by the Christian through the hypothesis that, being made in the image of God, he was given illumination to see more of the problem of epistemology than were others" (p. 186). With Plato, with Descartes, and with Kant, the "Conservative", as a follower of Augustine, would appeal to an innate knowledge of self that the rational man possesses and to a criterion that this rational man has within himself by which he may judge of the validity of any revelational claim (pp. 158 ff.; also p. 125).

Against all this the "Augustinianism" of Richardson has no complaint to make. When Carnell fails to distinguish clearly between the Augustinianism that has come to expression in Calvin and the Augustinianism that comes to expression in Descartes, he is playing into the hand of his foe. Calvin did, and Descartes did not, make the Creator-creature relation fundamental in his thought. Calvin did, and Descartes did not, make the fact of the fall of man determinative in his estimate of man himself. When Carnell's "Conservative" follows Calvin, he boldly contends that Scripture is the Christian's highest category. When this same "Conservative" follows Descartes, he virtually allows would-be autonomous reason to pass sentence both upon the credibility and the content of Scripture. The "Conservative" will need to choose between these two. But then it is endemic to the nature of the "Conservative", that is to an "Evangelical" who refuses frankly to confess Calvinism, to halt between two opinions. It is only on the basis of the Reformed Faith that a clear distinction can be made between Calvin and Descartes, between a true and a false Augustinianism. Arminian Evangelicalism, in practice, always tones down the Creator-creature distinction. Its doctrine of "free will" requires it to do so. The same holds true of the doctrine of sin. Accordingly it is quite impossible for Carnell's "Conservative" really to challenge the "Augustinianism" of Richardson on the matter of the criterion of judgment.

And here lies the fundamental weakness of Carnell's book. It is formally correct in its argument against all forms of mysticism and empiricism. Carnell is rightly anxious not to tie up Christianity with a theory of knowledge that cannot· distinguish between truth and "snarks, boojums, splinth, and gobble-de-gook" (p. 81). But why is Carnell not equally anxious to avoid tieing up Christianity with a theory of knowledge that would, forthwith, make impossible the idea of Biblical revelation itself? Christianity is squarely opposed to irrationalism; but it is equally opposed to rationalism. An *a priori* such as that of Plato, of Descartes, of Kant, or of Blanshard makes man himself the final reference point of all interpretation. Such an *a priori* requires that the contents of any "revelation" shall be poured into hard and fast moulds supposedly found within the human mind. Modern theology has obeyed the requirements of this *a priori* and has therefore cast overboard the doctrines of God's transcendence, of man's creation and fall, and every other doctrine of orthodox Christianity. It was only logical in doing so. Those theologians who have most consistently followed out the demands of the *a priori* of the men to whom Carnell makes his appeal have been the first to put Christianity on a par with "snarks, boojums, splinth, and gobble-de-gook".

It is not any *a priori*, but the specifically Christian *a priori*, that saves from scepticism. Traditional apologetics failed to point out this fact. In consequence, it found itself writhing in the clutches of its foes. In many other respects Carnell has left Thomas and Butler far behind. He rises to great heights when he boldly claims that only the Christian has the logical right to speak of anything at all. But then at the crucial point his "Conservative" crouches before the throne of the natural man offering to trim the contents of the Bible itself to any form and size required.

Apparently the "Conservative" leans heavily on the recent generosity of the natural man. Has not this natural man made a recent edict that henceforth he will not require the positive but only the negative application of the law of contradiction to the contents of any revelation? The "Conservative" apparently thinks that this edict gives standing to the uniqueness of the facts of Christianity. But he overlooks the fact that the uniqueness thus allowed is the uniqueness of irrationalism. From the high position where he claims: "In history, then, there is no surd, inexplicable, or antinomy. History is as rational at every point as the rational God Who decrees its movement" (p. 296), Carnell's "Conservative" descends to the admission that "all reality is obscure" (p. 209). From the high position where he claims that the promises of God with respect to the course of history cannot fail, this same "Conservative" descends to the plainest irrationalism when he says: "If the scientist cannot rise above rational probability in his empirical investigation, why should the Christian claim more?" (p. 114). The modern scientist is a cross between a rationalist and an irrationalist. As a rationalist his *a priori* principles require him to say with Spinoza that the order and connection of ideas is the same as the order and connection of things. Virtually making no distinction between the mind of God and the mind of man as God's creature, he must therefore seek to individuate by complete description. He may say that man reasons discursively and God knows intuitively but he cannot make this distinction mean anything in practice. On rationalist principles man either knows all things or he knows nothing.

The rationalist should be able to predict the whole course of history, except for the fact that on his basis the idea of prediction is meaningless. For him all historical factuality is identical with timeless logic.

To escape this nemesis the scientist also becomes irrationalist. He would save individual historical existence, but to do so he must posit an existence that is prior to, and independent of, all rationality. He therefore contends that space-time factuality is in the nature of the case obscure. He commits himself to a view of individuality diametrically opposed to that of Scripture.

Being both rationalist and irrationalist is to embrace the utterly self-contradictory and meaningless notion of *rational probability*. For facts to be rational means, on this basis, to be exhaustively, demonstratively, analytically or intuitively known. The facts must lose their existence to be known. Thus there is no probability; there is omniscience. On the other hand, if the facts retain their existence, they are utterly unknown. There is then no rationality; there is ignorance.

Why then should the "Conservative" appeal to this principle? If he "ardently defends a system of authority" (p. 71) he does so only because, in effect, he admits to his judge, the natural man, that the Christian hypothesis is, like any other hypothesis, a fish-line of rationality thrown out into a shoreless and bottomless ocean of Chance. Thus we are back to the "snarks".

In conclusion we repeat that Carnell's effort to reach a higher position in orthodox apologetics than that furnished by Aquinas and Butler is laudable indeed. But it is only when his "Conservative" learns to make his Calvinism count more consistently than he has in this book, that he can effectively meet the needs of our day. The modernist apologete is now pretty consistently pagan; the orthodox apologete must be consistently Christian. It is consistent Christianity, it is Calvinism, that alone can meet the scepticism of unbelief. Carnell's "Conservative" seems to believe this. Why does he not tell the world so?

ed. Vergilius Ferm: *A History of Philosophical Systems*. New York: The Philosophical Library. 1950. xvi, 642. $6.00.

The volume before us is the result of a cooperative enterprise. Various specialists have written brief articles on the field of their specialty. These articles together cover the whole field of the history of philosophy.

There is one obvious advantage of this method of dealing with the history of philosophy. It allows for a much wider range of interest than is possible for a book written by one author. There is greater justice done to such systems of philosophy as are written in foreign, and particularly in Oriental, languages. Then, too, there is greater justice done to such subjects as lie on the periphery of philosophy proper. So, for example, A. Cornelius Benjamin, an expert in the philosophy of the sciences, contributes an article on the field of his special interest. The same is true of the philosophy of religion. As his earlier publications show, the editor of this volume has for some time been much interested in this field. It is he who has written the article on this subject.

There is also one obvious disadvantage in the presentation of the history of philosophical systems by the method under consideration. There is no one philosophy of history that serves as a criterion for the evaluation of the various systems that are brought under review. If one reads a history of philosophy by Ruggiero, the Italian Idealist, one learns how Plato, Kant or Hegel looks from where Ruggiero sits. If one reads a history of philosophy by Vollenhoven, the Dutch Calvinist, one learns how Plato, Kant or Hegel looks as seen through Calvinistic eyes. Such unity of approach is naturally impossible by the present method. There is great variety and little unity.

It is quite impossible to deal with the content of all the various contributions to this book. Our interest may more profitably be centered on one or two articles that have a bearing on religion and particularly on Christianity. The editor himself writes an article on "Philosophies of Religion" and another on "Early Christian Philosophy". A few remarks may be made about each of these articles in turn.

In the former article Ferm bewails the fact that the subject of the philosophy of religion has so seldom been dealt with by those who are competent to carry on mature and disciplined inquiry (p. 598). Men have all too often worked "under the constraints of their own religious cultus" (p. 599). Indicating his own approach he says: "The field of the philosophy of religion may be defined as an inquiry into the general subject of religion without bias to any particular one, employing the tools of critical analysis and evaluation. It is a part of free philosophical inquiry using data from whatever source" (*idem*). And "even though the chorus in praise of 'faith' and 'communion' and 'authority' and 'revelation' is still strong" Ferm is confident that things will sooner or later improve "for the simple reason that reason itself is man's only way of ever coming to non-dogmatic terms with the world" (pp. 605 f.). When that happy day arrives, "religions will no longer seem divided into hard and fast divisions. All of them will be seen to be essentially plural, as plural as is the Christian religion in all its varieties" (p. 606).

If we were not accustomed to seeing men handle the "religious consciousness" of man in some such way as is suggested by Ferm we might be amazed at its utterly uncritical character. Together with many of his contemporaries the editor of this volume simply takes for granted that "reason" is the instrument of a perfectly normal man. It assumes that there is no such thing as sin as defined in terms of the Bible. How would Ferm go about *proving* that there is no such thing as sin? He doesn't bother to ask himself that question. He is not interested in "the more sombre features of Protestant orthodoxy" (p. 605). His "descriptive" method would not allow for the possibility that Protestant orthodoxy might be true. And this in spite of the fact that description pure and simple is impossible. A criterion of evaluation is always assumed by every one who thinks he merely describes the phenomena of the religious consciousness. It is not mere description but negative evaluation, and that on purely non-rational ground, which operates within the "reason" to which Ferm so confidently appeals. Is it this same non-rational attitude, or is it merely lack of acquaintance, that accounts for the absence of any reference to the Calvinistic philosophy of D. H. Th. Vollenhoven and H. Dooyeweerd?

The same bias that controls Ferm's method when dealing with the philosophy of religion also controls him when he deals with early Christian philosophy. It is to be expected that Tertullian should come in for some "neutral" description. "It was Marcionism that Tertullian denounced in five volumes of writings and, before that, all forms of heresies. Against them he took his stand upon the scriptures. To argue with authorities, he held, was to deny them. A philosopher is always in quest of something; the believer, on the other hand, has ended his quest even though what he believes may be absurd ... Thus did a spirit of antirationalism enter into Catholic orthodoxy and a rule of faith take the seat of honor" (p. 147).

It is apparently his unreasoned assumption of the normalcy and ultimacy of human reason and therefore his equally unreasoned hostility to "authority" that accounts for his inability to see any unity in the thought of St. Augustine. He cannot even find anything like a steady direction of development in Augustine's thought. Apparently impressed with the many-sided character of the genius of Augustine he, none the less, basically thinks of Augustine as unable to find integration in his thought. To Ferm it is evidence of dual or multiple personality if one holds to the possibility of a philosophy that takes the authority of Scripture into account. "There is no Augustinian 'system' for a very simple reason:

there is no one Augustine. His personality was a criss-cross of many currents, much like Paul before him, like Luther and George Fox after him" (p. 152). How is it possible that a man should be "at times a philosopher free to speculate and again a subject devoutly loyal to his tradition and church" (p. 153)? No better illustration could be given of how the supposedly scientific *description* of a philosopher of genius, like Augustine, turns out to be no description at all. The subject to be described disappears as he is being described. The student of this descriptive article does not as much as get a glimpse of the greatest of Christian philosophers. But then it is assumed that those who are Christians cannot engage in rational inquiry; the student must take this on the authority of Ferm.

S. J. Ridderbos: *De Theologische Cultuurbeschouwing van Abraham Kuyper*. Kampen: J. H. Kok. 1947. 338.

I. A. Diepenhorst: *Algemeene Genade en Antithese*. Kampen: J. H. Kok. 1947. 52. Fl. 0.80 (paper).

These two publications here brought to the notice of the reader deal with the Christian philosophy of culture as this has found expression in recent Reformed theology, and particularly in the works of Abraham Kuyper.

Romanists have frequently charged that because of its low view of human reason Reformed theology is unable to account for the accomplishments of science and art. In reply to this and other such charges, Kuyper pointed out that in reality it is only in terms of Reformed theology that one can account for culture. For Reformed theology is Christianity come to its own. The more truly Biblical one's conception of God and man the more truly can one account for human culture. But what of the doctrine of total depravity? Does not that depreciate all human accomplishment? Not at all, says Kuyper. To teach total depravity is also to teach the grace of God. It is by the grace of God that men, though sinners, may yet build the structure of human culture. There is, first, saving grace. It is that by which men strive self-consciously to do all things to the glory of God. It is that which enables them to engage in artistic and scientific construction as well as in worship, never forgetting the fact that they are building the temple of God.

But there is also common grace. It does not change the heart of man. But it restrains him from spending all his energies in building a tower of Babel. And while restraining the downward and destructive tendency of sin, it even enables him to labour conjointly with the believer in bringing to light the potentialities of God's created universe. Thus it is that the Reformed theology, with its doctrine of total depravity complemented by its teaching of grace, both special and common, is able to show that Christianity and it alone saves man, the whole man, for this life as well as for the one that is to come.

Ridderbos has done a fine service in bringing together the materials that bear on Kuyper's conception of human culture. It enables one afresh to rejoice in the comprehensive and balanced character of the Reformed Faith. It enables one to realize anew how it is only in Reformed thinking that one can explain the whole of human experience.

But this is not to say that Reformed theology has come to a fully adequate expression of Christian truth. Reformed theologians are fully aware of this fact. One problem that vexes them greatly is that of the relation of special to common grace. Some have even found them irreconcilable. Such is the case with H. Hoeksema. Others have found it necessary to re-evaluate Kuyper's statement of the relationship between the two. They have felt themselves compelled to reduce the significance of common grace lest it should, after all, impinge upon the purity of the doctrine of special grace which all are equally anxious to maintain. Among these are such men as de Graaf, Dooyeweerd and Schilder.

Ridderbos, however, is inclined to leave Kuyper's structure intact. He likes the old mansion pretty much as it is.

We are inclined to think that in this he is too optimistic. We do not agree with Hoeksema in thinking that Kuyper's mansion needs to be destroyed. But we do think that it needs a new roof.

We do not know why Ridderbos failed to take notice of the criticisms by Hoeksema of Kuyper's view of common grace. These criticisms are as fundamental as any that are lodged by the theologians he discusses. Even so, Ridderbos does not succeed too well in answering some of the criticisms of Kuyper that he considers. One such point may here be indicated.

The chief task of human culture, Kuyper argues, is the development of the potentialities God has placed in the created world (Ridderbos, p. 287). At the same time Kuyper contends that it is through common grace that mankind can fulfill this task. "Thanks to common grace the powers of creation come to fruition in spite of sin. And this preserving and development of the original creation to the glory of God, is the first, independent goal of common grace" (p. 89). Accordingly the covenant of God with Noah is said to be a covenant with man as man. It is to enable man as man, whether believer or unbeliever, to fulfill his cultural task.

But is it not man's business to do all things self-consciously to the glory of God? And are the recipients of common, but not of special, grace in covenant with God to do all things to His glory? Or, if not, is their task really fulfilled if with grouchy faces, as driven workers in God's concentration camp, they carry their brick-and mortar? All that is not of faith is sin. If non-believers do help for the fulfilling of man's task, they do so in spite of themselves, because they could not even be successful as covenant-breakers if they were not also forced to be, in spite of themselves, co-labourers with God's covenant-keepers. But then, to bring out this fact, the covenant with Noah should have been made subordinate to the covenant of grace with Abraham. True, Kuyper says that the common grace has a second goal, the goal of preparing the ground for special grace. But this should be its *only* purpose. True also, Kuyper says that both purposes of common grace must serve the glory of God (pp. 92 f.). But the devils also must serve the glory of God. And in their hearts unbelievers are in covenant with Satan. To the extent that they are conscious of this fact they would destroy all culture. Their "coöperation on common ground" with believers in the construction of human culture is possible because they are not fully conscious of their own basic principles. And the Christian can accept of this coöperation only if he is himself fully aware of the difference in ultimate objectives that obtains between the unbeliever and himself in *all* that they do.

Kuyper's work on common grace needs reconstruction along these lines. To speak of an independent goal of common grace is to tone down to some extent the claim of Christianity as alone being able to save.

It is therefore also to tone down the difference between the Roman Catholic and the Reformed conceptions of human culture.

Ridderbos seems to be unwilling to face this fact. His work, admirable as it is in many ways, resembles that of a man who has just a few, say three or four, new shingles with which to repair a leaky roof. He uses the new shingles for the largest holes, but insists on re-using all the old shingles for the smaller leaks. With considerable ingenuity he trims as he replaces but the result is, at best, a makeshift. It is no dishonor to a father who has built a house if the son finds that fifty years later it needs a new roof.

A brief word may be added about Diepenhorst's pamphlet. Its title indicates that it is designed to deal with the specific question of the relation of the doctrine of total depravity and common grace. Diepenhorst does take notice of Hoeksema's criticism of Kuyper. He also concedes, implicitly if not always explicitly, that Kuyper's views on common grace need considerable modification. In particular, Kuyper's insistence on the independent goal of common grace has virtually disappeared. Diepenhorst merely denies the *exclusive* subservience of common to special grace. And the reason given is the perfectly innocent one that God may rejoice Himself in the glories of nature never seen by man. For the rest, he maintains as the central and main purpose of common grace that it serve the purposes of redemption (p. 19).

Even so, Diepenhorst does not really come to grips with the most basic criticism made of Kuyper. As already indicated above, that criticism has placed Reformed theologians before the responsibility of articulating their various teachings more self-consciously in relation to one another. When they are confronted with such teachings as are found in Romans 1:20 and 2:14,15 they will have to distinguish their position carefully from that of Scholasticism. Scholasticism confuses the ever present pressure of God's revelational requirement upon man with the sinner's ethical response to this revelation. From the fact that every man knows God and His law, because he cannot escape knowing Him, Romanism concludes that every sinner has, at points, a proper reaction to this knowledge. It is on this confusion that the Roman Catholic conception of natural theology is based. Rome teaches that the reason of man as such, whether or not he be regenerate, does interpret something of God's revelation truly. What Reformed theologians are now seeking to do is to show that any true interpretation on the part of the natural man is due to the fact that he is not a finished product, that he has been unable to suppress God's revelation within and about him completely.

Kuyper failed to stress this point. He frequently spoke of *areas* or *territories* of activity that believers and unbelievers have in common. As though there were any commonness without difference. There is need for commonness. Kuyper was right in stressing this fact. Christianity is truly human and Christian culture is the only truly human culture. But the commonness required by Christian culture is commonness with a difference. Would that Diepenhorst had joined the constructive critics of Kuyper in making plain this fact. Then his otherwise masterful control of all the factors that bear on the subject would have been made to serve a still better purpose than it has.

J. J. Louët Feisser: *De Strijd Tegen de Analogia Entis in de Theologie van Karl Barth*. Amsterdam: Uitgeverij H. J. Paris. 1948. XII, 107.

We have before us a doctoral dissertation presented at the University of Utrecht. Its title would lead one to expect a discussion of Karl Barth's debate with Erich Przywara and Roman Catholicism in general. We are not disappointed in finding that such is not the case. Feisser deals with a broader and more basic problem. He is concerned with Barth's general Christological approach to the problems of theology. It is Barth's radically kenotic Christology, says Feisser, that makes him reject not only the Roman Catholic, but also the traditional Protestant, view of analogy. Barth is not merely opposed to Romanists who hold to a natural theology constructed by reason and add to it a theology based on revelation. He is even more opposed to Protestants who, though they reject natural theology, none the less deny the hidden character of God's revelation (p. 68). His opposition is therefore directed as much against Calvin as against Romanism. It is not a question of this doctrine or of that. It is rather a question of a totally different outlook on theology as a whole. From Barth's point of view Calvin fails to see that the *Deus Revelatus* is as such the *Deus Absconditus* (p. 13). Accordingly Calvin builds up a *locus de Deo* in which he presupposes an analogy between God and man such as Barth would reject (*idem*). Barth, to be sure, speaks of analogy between God and man but this analogy consists of a union between two wholly diverse entities (p. 14). This makes "hiddenness" the hallmark of revelation itself. More recently Herman Bavinck has represented Calvin's point of view (p. 16). In line with Calvin's thought Bavinck speaks of God as having revealed himself in the created universe. That is, he speaks not only of the act of God's creation but also of the finished result of that act as confronting man and enabling him, as God's image-bearer, to obtain ectypal knowledge of God. In all this Bavinck lays the foundation for his doctrine of the incarnation (p. 20). A true Barthian, says Feisser, will be terrified by such a *theologia gloriae*. There is a deep rift between the theology of Bavinck and that of Barth (p. 21). In his *Kirchliche Dogmatik* III, 1, Barth works out fully his Christological conception of creation (p. 30). Christologically interpreted the image of God in man is never a quality (p. 36). To bear the image of God is to be *open for* the grace of God (p. 39). Therefore man's sin is his opposition to the grace of God. It is to destroy his openness toward God; it is to fall back upon himself, that is upon nothing (p. 40). Barth's theology must therefore be regarded as being not merely a "correction" or modification of neo-Calvinism but as a radical break with Calvin and the Reformation itself (p.42). Feisser speaks of an "astounding lack of critical discrimination", both on the part of Barth's friends and of his critics, in failing to see the radical difference between the Theology of Crisis and the theology of the Reformation (p. 72).

In the last part of his book, Feisser seeks to safeguard the Theology of Crisis against a common misunderstanding. We are not to think of Barth as first speaking of God as hidden in order after that to speak of this hidden God as revealing himself. On the contrary we know nothing of God except through his revelation in Christ. Barth would begin with the revelation of God in Christ. It is from this revelation itself that we learn that God is hidden. Thus we have not Kantianism but inverted Kantianism (p. 85). This approach enables Barth to speak much more positively of the fulness of the grace of God than the Reformers did.

Feisser's dissertation is, we believe, a valuable contribution to the literature dealing with the Theology of Crisis. If one accepts the main principle of Barth's theology, one must reject the main principle of Reformation theology. To show how both friends and critics of Barth frequently forget this fact is to help clarify the theological atmosphere. But why then does Feisser obscure his own main contention by frequently speaking as though Barth and the Reformers meant the same thing after all?

Feisser himself confuses the issue when he deals with the doctrine of creation. He points to Barth's *Kirchliche Dogmatik* III,1 in which, he says, Barth has, with thorough consistency, interpreted creation along christological lines (p. 30). He then speaks of the "fearful misunderstanding" of Berkouwer, who criticises Barth for leveling off or obscuring the historical relationship between creation and the fall. But in all this Feisser fails to assert his own main principle. Why did he not point out that since Barth and Reformed theology have a radically different view of God and of man, it is confusing to speak, as Berkouwer does, of a leveling off of *the historical relation* between creation and the fall in the case of Barth? In the volume to which Feisser refers (III, 2), and in particular in the second part of that volume, Barth sets forth at length the radical difference between his view of history and that of traditional Reformation theology. For Barth the story of creation is *reine Saga* (III, 1, p. 89). To be sure, he would distinguish *Saga* from *Mythus*. The latter he defines as an illustration of a timeless truth, while the former refers to real history (*Geschichte*). But Barth is very careful to distinguish his view of *Geschichte* from the traditional view of history. Did he not many years ago ask "the dear friends of the speaking serpent" in Utrecht to be concerned rather about *what* the serpent spoke than about *whether* there was a real serpent that spoke? That remark of Barth's was directed against the theologians of the Reformed Churches in The Netherlands, who had recently deposed Dr. Geelkerken because he did not hold to the historicity of the Genesis account. In similar fashion, and with no less pathos, Barth is doubly careful now to point out that real history as he holds to it (*Geschichte* as *reine Saga*), is not to be identified with *historische Geschichte*, with history such as traditional theology insists on holding (III, 1, p. 84). Why then did not Feisser point out that the weakness of Berkouwer's criticism of Barth lay in the fact that he spoke of Barth's confusing *the* historical relation of the creation and the fall? How can there be a toning down of *the* historical relation between creation and the fall in Barth's theology, if he does not believe in the historicity of either creation or the fall? From the orthodox point of view, Barth has rejected historic Christianity in its entirety. From Barth's point of view, orthodox Christianity has rejected the true historic (*geschichtliche*) character of Christianity entirely. It is this fact that Feisser's own principle should have made him bring into operation as against Berkouwer. As it is he fails to do so (p. 41).

In passing, we note that Feisser again fails to apply his own principle when he speaks of the Barthian and the Reformation doctrines of justification. He speaks as though there were basic agreement on the forensic character of this doctrine (p. 59). And this in spite of the fact that in the immediate context he once more signalises the basic difference between the Reformation and the dialectical concepts of revelation (p. 63).

Perhaps the most striking failure to apply his own principle is found in Feisser's dealing with the concept of grace. Here would have been his best opportunity to establish the truth of his main contention. Why did he not show how radically different are the two conceptions of grace, that held by Barth and that held by Reformation theology? Here, if anywhere, the difference between Barth's doctrine of the *Deus Revelatus* as being the *Deus Absconditus* and the Reformation doctrine of God's direct and finished revelation in Scripture is apparent. The difference lies primarily in the fact that, for Barth, God's *No* is always penultimate, never ultimate. God's wrath is always wrath in Christ. His punishment is always exclusively remedial. "Man is the being to whom God is gracious" (III, 2, p. 39). Man's being consists in his being with Christ and therefore with God (III, 2, p. 161). Man's real choice, his real freedom, consists, therefore, in choosing *for* God. His choice against God is not a real possibility at all. For Barth, this is the essence of his Christological foundation for anthropology. He rejects every anthropology, even that of Brunner, in which man's choice against God is presented as an ultimate rather than as a penultimate possibility (III, 2, p. 157). Man exists truly only if and to the extent that he chooses for Christ. It is therefore safe to say that no "theology" has been devised by modern man that more thoroughly and completely rejects the Reformation teaching with respect to the grace of God than does the theology of Barth. Feisser speaks quite rightly of the relentless consistency with which Barth has applied his main principle in his major discussion of anthropology. Is it then only to speak "much more positively than the Reformation of the fulness of living by the grace of God", when Barth identifies man's true existence itself as existence in grace? Feisser speaks as though the Reformation and Barth are essentially at one in their conception of the meaning of the grace of God in Christ.

Perhaps the reason why Feisser is unable to carry through his own principle consistently is the fact that, after all, he regards both the Reformation and the Barthian theologies as two forms of Christian theology. He is, after all, unwilling to make a final choice between them. His sympathies are obviously with Barth. Apparently he has quite misunderstood Barth's main principle after all. Feisser is no doubt formally correct when he says that according to Barth we must start with God's revelation in Christ. God is for Barth identical with his revelation in Christ. But man is also identical with his revelation to himself in Christ. The God and the man of Barth become what they are because of their common relation to Christ. They *become* what they are in Christ; they are what they are because of a common *Geschichte*. Man *participates* in the history of Christ. He exists to the extent that he participates in this history. And this history is the history of redemption. Man exists to the extent that he participates in Christ's redemptive work for all and every man. Man exists to the extent that he is the co-redemptor with Christ of mankind.

Such is the main argument of Barth's anthropology. Feuerbach has better reasons than ever to look down upon this most modern form of "theology" as nothing but undercover humanistic anthropology. It is not difficult to imagine him attacking the *Church Dogmatics* of Barth with even more glee than he did *The Christian Faith* of Schleiermacher in order to show that both its God and its Christ are nothing but hypostatized projections of man's ideal of himself as a wonderful person, trying his best to help all men everywhere to more noble living. Barth's theology is humanism of the purest water; it has not a drop of grace in it as the Reformation understood grace. It is this fact that needs pointing out. Feisser's dissertation at first encourages us in thinking that it is this point that he intends to make clear, but, after all, he falls into the all-too-common habit of confusing the issue between orthodox theology and the Theology of Crisis.

K. Schilder: *Christus in zijn Lijden.* Kampen: J. H. Kok N. V. Second Edition. Vol. I — *Christus aan den Ingang van zijn Lijden.* 1949. 584. Fl. 13.25. Vol. II — *Christus in den Doorgang van zijn Lijden.* 1951. 619. Fl. 13.75.

The first edition of Dr. Schilder's work on the passion of Christ appeared in 1929. An English translation was published by Wm. B. Eerdmans Publishing Co. under the titles *Christ in His Suffering* (1938), *Christ on Trial* (1939), and *Christ Crucified* (1940).

The first two volumes of the second edition, enlarged and greatly enriched, are now at hand. The third volume is soon to appear. A review of the first edition was published in this *Journal* by Professor R. B. Kuiper. A short notice must now suffice.

In reading Schilder's work some familiar words of B. B. Warfield on Calvinism came to mind again. Said Warfield: "In it, objectively speaking, theism comes to its rights; subjectively speaking, the religious relation attains its purity; soteriologically speaking, evangelical religion finds at length its full expression and its secure stability" (*Calvin as a Theologian and Calvinism To-day*, Philadelphia, 1909, p. 23).

The great and sovereign God, creator of the world, and ultimate determiner of man's destiny, stands at the center of Schilder's thought. Theism comes to its own. This sovereign God speaks through the Word as infallibly written by prophets and apostles. With unexcelled penetration this Word is made to bear upon man in all the fulness of his responsibilities. The religious relation attains to its purity. The same sovereign God, in and through the incarnate Word, founds his kingdom on his substitutionary death and resurrection, thus utterly defeating the kingdom and the power of Satan. Evangelical religion finds at length its full expression. Here is reformed, and therefore biblical, piety at its very best.

D. H. Th. Vollenhoven: *Geschiedenis der Wijsbegeerte*. Vol. I. Franeker: T. Wever. 1950. 621 + chart. Fl. 25.00.

Dr. Vollenhoven is well known as the brilliant and erudite professor of philosophy at the Free University of Amsterdam. Together with his colleague, Dr. H. Dooyeweerd, he has developed a truly Christian, that is, a frankly Calvinistic, view of philosophy. Contrary to all other schools of philosophy, which they signalize as immanentistic, these men presuppose the truth of God's special redemptive revelation to man in the Scriptures of the Old and New Testaments. It is their contention that unless one presupposes the view of reality and knowledge authoritatively set forth in Scripture one's philosophical research is bound to issue in hopeless antinomies.

Naturally such a view of philosophy calls for a rewriting of the history of philosophy. The ordinary textbook on the history of philosophy presupposes an immanentistic theory of being and knowledge. Over against the usual type of text-book (including those proceeding from Roman Catholic writers) Vollenhoven is writing a history of philosophy from an avowedly Christian point of view.

If one should conclude from these remarks that the author's project deals with the philosophy of history rather than with the history of philosophy a real surprise awaits him. There is such a wealth of historical detail found in Vollenhoven's volume as is seldom seen elsewhere. The author has made an exhaustive study of the extant "fragments" and documents bearing on the beginnings of Greek speculations. There is before us in this volume the ripe result of historical research of the first order.

There are surprising and challenging contentions made in this book. Have you not been summarising the thought of Heraclitus with the expression *panta rhei*? If you have, then you have been following the "usual" interpretation of Heraclitus. But this usual interpretation, Vollenhoven argues, is not justified by the fragments. How then would he signalize the thought of Heraclitus? It is impossible to indicate this unless I should restate the basic schematism according to which he arranges the various schools of philosophy. And this cannot be done in a brief review or note. Equally challenging assertions are made about Parmenides, Anaxagoras, and other pre-Socratics.

This schematism is not easy to understand. It is exceedingly, if not excessively, complex. A large chart, snugly deposited at the end of the book, gives a survey of the history of Greek philosophy, according to the general schematism adopted.

The reader will notice that we have before us the first volume of a projected series of books. Vollenhoven hopes to publish nine volumes in all, covering the history of philosophy down to date. He aspires thus to carry out a program announced in an earlier work, *Het Calvinisme en de Reformatie van de Wijsbegeerte* (1933).

The undertaking is a truly prodigious one. But the learning and industry already displayed in the earlier volume, as well as in the work herewith brought to the attention of the reader, makes one hopeful of the final completion of it all.

The usefulness of the present volume for apologetical purposes can scarcely be overestimated. Christian apologetics needs to trace the devious paths by which the natural man has sought to suppress the truth within and about him. Only by understanding the various forms assumed by the enemy will the Christian apologete be able to set forth the truth clearly against falsehood. A history of philosophy, written from a fully Christian point of view, written by one who knows and believes Calvinism as Christianity come to its own, and written by a man of astounding erudition in the field of philosophy, is making its appearance in our day. It is an event of the first magnitude.

L. W. Grensted: *The Psychology of Religion.* New York: Oxford University Press. 1952. vii, 181. $3.00.

As a science the Psychology of Religion has been with us since the turn of the century. Those who worked in the field had high expectations for it. They hoped to find at last the clue to the "nature of religion". It would be possible now, as never before, to ask men to say frankly, without inhibitions, what religion meant to them. Formerly men had been kept from speaking the deep meanings of their hearts. They were told what they had to say. They were repressed by systems of theology and metaphysics. But now, like children released from the instructions of their parents, they could give forth their "native witness". Questionnaires were quickly drawn up. Hindus, Mohammedans, Christians and many others were asked to speak freely on the question, What does religion mean to me? The gathering of a great mass of facts was surely the first step for a scientist to take.

Trouble sprang up when the second, and equally inevitable, step had to be taken. The facts had to be screened. Surely some religions were better than others. It was held that to look for "religion as such" would require no accumulation of opinions. Religion *as such* can be found by any one in an armchair. One needs only to drop all positive opinions expressed by any one about the nature of religion. When one has reached a perfect blank then one has religion as such. But this negative and abstract procedure was fit for the rationalists of the eighteenth century. And this is the twentieth century. We must proceed concretely now. So we must, like the bees, gather our honey from far and near. Yet having gathered positive opinions we must ourselves pronounce positive judgments about the relative value of the various religions investigated. Are the head-hunters *wrong*? Or do they represent a *lower* view of religion? If as a Christian you make either of these judgments then you have forsaken your neutrality. You have re-introduced authority, your own or that of the suburb in which you live. You might as well have saved yourself the trouble of sending out a questionnaire; you could just as well ask yourself the question, "What do I mean by religion?" and stop at that point.

Of course the results of the questionnaire might comfort you. You have become entangled in a hopeless dilemma. You have gathered facts. You have explained facts but in explaining them you have explained them away or returned them unexplained. But others, you find, are faced with the same difficulty. Psychology in general, even philosophy, you discover, faces the same hopeless and self-contradictory situation. So, with them, you assume that such is, of necessity, the human predicament. Certainly then no one is to blame.

Christians may be tempted to find comfort in the fact that such a work as lies before us, by an outstandingly able man like Grensted, is opposed to the openly expressed hostility to Christianity of Freud, of Watson, of

Leuba and others. Particularly they may be tempted to console themselves by the repeated assertions of Grensted to the effect that his science deals with "religious behaviour", not with the reality of religion itself. They may even be tempted to take heart when they learn from the present work, and from others by the same author, that he himself believes in the reality of religion.

The real importance of the work of Grensted, however, lies in the fact that it exhibits in thorough fashion how in spite of his expressed phenomenalism and neutrality, in spite of his personal profession of religion, he has committed himself to a method that involves both by assumption and conclusion the absurdity of the claim of Christianity to be *the true* religion. The equation of Christianity with other religions is presupposed at the outset. Christianity claims to be true and as such to offer the only possible criterion of truth. Grensted starts by taking Christianity off this pedestal and setting it among all other religions as their equal. Then he looks for a criterion apart from and above Christianity by which to judge of its claim to be true. He judges of this claim by ignoring it, by assuming that the alternative of true and false must be replaced by that of the adequacy of the concept of religion. And yet this adequacy of concept turns out, on inspection, to be nothing but a matter of taste. *De gustibus non est disputandum.*

All this is not to depreciate Grensted's book as a work of scholarship. The book gives an admirable survey of the half century of work done by the science he so ably represents. Grensted holds to a moderate and balanced point of view; he gives the best that can be given on his basis.

Many valuable lessons may be learned from such works as that of the present writer. The "behavior of religion" as studied by the psychology of religion, is bound, in spite of the basic dilemma referred to, to be helpful in the study of both true and false religion.

But it is for Christians to realize that there is a repression deeper than can be sensed by all the "repressions" employed by the psychology of religion, taken by and large. It is the repression of the distinction between true and false religion so effectively accomplished by the assumptions of the psychology of religion. It is only when the "repressions" employed by the psychology of religion are interpreted in terms of this deeper repression that the "positive values" of this modern science can be gathered in.

REVIEWS OF BOOKS

David S. Cairns: *The Image of God in Man.* New York: Philosophical Library. 1953. 256. $4.50.

Modern man is asking about himself in recent times. He has become a puzzle to himself. His interpretations of his environment have led him to an impasse. Seeking to know everything, he wonders whether he knows anything. Is the trouble, perhaps, in himself? Has he, unawares, introduced so much of himself into the picture that objectivity has disappeared?

Theologians are trying to answer this question. They call men back to Christianity. Christianity, they say, can tell man what he is. And knowing who and what he is, he can safely trust himself. Is he not a creature of God? Is he not made in the image of God? Without God he is a mystery to himself; with God he knows himself and the world too.

It is to show the relevance of the biblical doctrine of man to the modern scene that Dr. Cairns writes his book.

By and large his position, he tells us, is very similar to that of Emil Brunner, and, to a lesser degree, like that of Karl Barth. Like both of these dialectical theologians, his aim is to give a "christological" interpretation of man.

Only by means of a truly biblical or christological principle is it possible, he thinks, to find unity between the Old Testament and the New Testament picture of man.

On the surface the Old Testament and the New Testament teachings about man seem to conflict (pp. 29 f.). Yet in reality, "the fundamental conceptions of the New Testament are the legitimate descendants of those in the Old Testament" (p. 55). For by means of this principle it becomes apparent that the Old Testament concept of the image of God in man, based upon the gift of God in creation, is subordinate to the New Testament concept which entails God's ultimate purpose for man.

Moreover, when we take our position in the christological principle the biblical view in its entirety can be set off clearly from all non-biblical conceptions. "In our opinion . . . the personal relation of the Creator to his creature is fundamental, and any power of reason given to the created person is secondary to this" (p. 63). The doctrine of creation provides a foundation for that of revelation. It shows that man's knowledge is analogical; it cannot penetrate the essence of God. Yet man's knowledge is true because it comes from God. No form of identity philosophy can assert this much (*idem*). Human reason is not a spark of the divine fire, " 'a piece drawn off from Zeus' ", " 'an emanation of him who administers the universe' " or a " 'god dwelling as guest in the human frame' " (p. 62).

To the doctrine of creation must be added that of sin (p. 69). When we take the doctrines of creation and of sin as our starting point, regarding them christologically, then the relevance of the Christian view of man to our times becomes apparent. We then do justice to the fact that "man is always with God; confronted by Him". On the other hand we can then do justice to the fact that "man's being cannot be understood apart from the divine election; God's purpose of salvation for him" (*idem*).

The history of the doctrine of the image of God in man is there to warn us of certain danger points. Failing to do full justice to the difference between creation and emanation, some men overstressed the continuity between God and man. Or, failing to do justice to the fact that by virtue of creation man is always related to God and the object of his favor, some men have overstressed the discontinuity between God and man. So, for instance, St. Augustine, though fully declaring our "inability to save ourselves" yet in his doctrine of the image "has taken over just so much from non-Christian thought as will influence the course of his teaching from time to time, and make him suggest a capacity for self-salvation by an interior process of reflection" (p. 98). St. Thomas Aquinas, in particular, taking over "with too little modification the Aristotelian way of thinking" (p. 117), builds his structure of grace in too simple and positive a fashion upon that of nature (*idem*). It was in the Reformation that the true dialectical or christological principle first began to control the formulation of the idea of God's image in man (p. 127).

But while rightly taking the New Testament concept of the image as fundamental, Calvin was "faced with the problem of relating it to the Old Testament image, which is common to all mankind" (p. 132). Fortunately, Calvin stressed the principle of continuity as well as that of discontinuity. While holding that the image of God is lost through sin (p. 132), he yet speaks of "relics" of that image by which man continues to be confronted with God (p. 136). There is, according to Calvin, " 'more worth in all the vermin in the world than in man' " for " 'there is nothing in him but sin; we have so gone to the devil, and he does not only govern us, but has us in his possession, he is our prince' " (quoted on p. 139). On the other hand in his doctrine of the "relic", he holds that much of true morality and knowledge is found among men.

But Calvin was unable to find a proper working relation between his principle of discontinuity and his principle of continuity. His doctrine of election (discontinuity) kept him from properly asserting the universal character (continuity) of God's plan of salvation for man. "For the real link between the universal Old Testament image and the New Testament image, which is the hope of men in Christ, is the loving purpose of all men through Him" (p. 144). "The middle term which gives unity to the image is thus faulty or missing in Calvin's theology. If it be urged that if we reject Calvin's view of election, then we must either accept universalism, or believe that God's will for men may in some cases be finally thwarted; the point will have to be conceded" (p. 145).

The argument of Cairns is similar to that of Barth and Brunner. A truly balanced combination of the principles of continuity and discontinuity can be obtained, he reasons, only if one uses the dialectical rather than the historic Christian methodology. A truly dialectical or christological principle of continuity provides for the idea that all men are ultimately image bearers of God because they are in Christ. Their unity with Christ is to be eschatologically conceived. With Brunner, Cairns holds that "original righteousness does not lie in the empirical time-series somewhere in the past" (p. 153). So also the principle of discontinuity, of the fall is "to be found, not in the region of the empirically ascertainable, but 'behind' it, not indeed in a timeless existence, or an existence above time, but in a created original existence, which, like the Creation, can only be 'seen' from the standpoint of the Word of God, and not from that of experience" (pp. 154 f.).

By thus lifting Christianity out of the realm of ordinary history we have, thinks Cairns, a position more true to Scripture and common sense (p. 127). With this evaluation we cannot agree. On the contrary, we hold the historic Christian view, and, in particular, the view of Calvin, to be biblical and therefore also according to common sense.

True, Cairns has well pointed out that in Calvin's combination of the principles of continuity and discontinuity no full systematic clarity has been obtained. To say this is not to agree with Brunner and Cairns that Calvin's "doctrine of the relic" "says both too much and too little. Too much, because it indicates that there remains in our nature an undamaged spot; and too little, because it forgets that even in our sin we bear witness to our original relationship to God" (p. 158). Calvin's "doctrine of the relic" implies no "undamaged spots" in our nature. On the other hand, his doctrine of total depravity presupposes that all sin is sin against God and is therefore actual only because of man's, even the sinner's, unavoidable confrontation with God. Even so, no exhaustively systematic relation is obtained by Calvin. We may well speak of "problems for Calvinists" on this point. But it must be remembered that it is of the essence of the Reformed view that a truly biblical system is analogical. It would do justice to all the facts of Scripture and organize them as far as possible. But since God's relation to man is, at every point, inexhaustively rich, man's logical powers are constantly confronted with the necessity of bowing to mystery as revealed in Scripture.

It is here that historic Reformed theology and modern dialecticism part. Modern dialecticism aims at exhaustive explanation. It wants a principle of continuity that lights up all of reality by the logic of man. It is this idea that is basic to its "christological principle". By means of this principle God is said to be exhaustively revealed to man in Christ as man is exhaustively revealed to God in Christ.

On the other hand, dialecticism subjects God along with man to a common principle of discontinuity. God as well as man dies.

Then the utterly rationalistic principle of continuity and the utterly irrationalistic principle of discontinuity are regarded as correlative to one another. They are nicely kept in balance. This scheme of correlativisms between abstract identity and abstract difference is imposed upon Scripture. Thus modern dialecticism in philosophy becomes "christological" in theology.

In all of this, however, biblical truth is honored only by lip-service. And "common sense" is no longer in evidence. For the correlativity between the irrationalism and the rationalism of modern thought, when thus put in theological garb, is but the embodiment of hopeless scepticism. The "Christ" of dialecticism cannot be identified. The "christological" principle through which salvation for man is to be effected is both "wholly known" when "wholly unknown" and "wholly unknown" when "wholly known". The simplicity of Scripture has been ignored and common sense set aside.

CURRENT PUBLICATIONS

MACK PUBLISHING COMPANY

The Atonement—A. A. Hodge/Hugh Martin $6.00

The Church of Christ—James Bannerman (2 Vols.) $12.00

The Westminster Assembly and its Work—B. B. Warfield $5.50

The Saviour of the World—B. B. Warfield $5.50

The Abrahamic Covenant in the Gospels—Theophilus Herter $6.00

*The Role of Women in the Church—Wayne Mack $1.25

*The Bible's Answer to the Question:
What is a Christian?—Wayne Mack S.50

The Revelation of St. John—E. W. Hengstenberg (2 Vols.) S12.00

The Kingdom of God
Under the Old Testament—E. W. Hengstenberg (2 Vols.) $12.00

The Psalms—E. W. Hengstenberg (3 Vols.) $16.50

Christ and the Scriptures—Adolph Saphir $4.50

Christianity in Modern Theology—Cornelius Van Til $1.50

Christianity and Idealism—Cornelius Van Til $2.00

Is This Really the End?—George Miladin $1.25

Baptism: Sacrament of the Covenant of Grace—P. Marcel $5.50

Order from

PURITAN– The Christian Bookshop
12 Forrest Rd.,
Edinburgh EH1 2QN
Tel. 031-225-6937
ok Service

*Also available from the Faith Reformed Baptist Church, 110 State Rd., Media, Pa.